CONTROVERSIES IN ELT

Also from LinguaBooks

The European Journal of Applied Linguistics and TEFL (EJALTEFL)

A refereed academic publication (appears twice yearly)

Edited by Andrzej Cirocki

Academic Presenting and Presentations

A preparation course for university students

Peter Levrai and Averil Bolster

<u>Shortlisted for the 2016 ELTon Award for Innovation in Learner Resources</u>

In A Strange Land

Short stories for creative learning

Andrzej Cirocki and Alicia Peña Calvo

The Fractal Approach to Teaching English as a Foreign Language

Dynamism and Change in ELT

Maurice Claypole

Teaching EFL Online

An e-moderator's report

Andrew R. Webster

EFL Communication Strategies in Second Life

An exploratory study

Susan Gowans

www.linguabooks.com

CONTROVERSIES IN ELT

What you always wanted to know about teaching English
but were afraid to ask

MAURICE CLAYPOLE

Controversies in ELT
What you always wanted to know about teaching English but were afraid to ask

Maurice Claypole has asserted his right under the Copyright, Designs and Patents Act, 1988 to be identified as the author of this work.

Copyright © 2010 Maurice Claypole

Second edition 2016

ISBN: 978-1-911369-00-4

A CIP catalogue record for this book is available from the British Library.

Published by LinguaBooks

www.linguabooks.com

Second Life® and Linden Lab® are registered trademarks of Linden Research, Inc.; AGC® Electroforming System is a registered trademark of Wieland Dental + Technik GmbH & Co KG; Hot Potatoes™ is a trademark of Half-Baked Software Inc.; Camtasia Studio® is a registered trademark of TechSmith Corporation; Skype™ is a registered trademark of Skype Limited. Further copyright holders are credited in the text or listed in the acknowledgments on p. 124. Every effort has been made to trace the holders of intellectual property rights and the publishers will be happy to correct mistakes or omissions in future editions.

The images on pages 56 and 93 were created using the Wordle.net application at http://www.wordle.net.

Cover photo (by the author): Sunset over the Lac Du Der

All rights reserved. No part of this publication may be reproduced, stored in a retrieval system or transmitted, in any form or by any means, electronic, mechanical, photocopying, recording or otherwise, without the prior permission of the publishers.

This book is sold subject to the condition that it shall not, by way of trade or otherwise, be lent, re-sold, hired out or otherwise circulated without the publisher's prior consent in any form of binding or cover other than that in which it is published and without a similar condition including this condition being imposed on the subsequent purchaser.

*For last year's words belong to last year's language
And next year's words await another voice.*

– T. S. Eliot, Little Gidding

Maurice Claypole BA MA (Lond), Cert Ed, MCIL, MCollT, AITI, PhD was born in Halifax, UK and now lives in Germany, where he and his wife Ann run a private language school and translation agency. One day he will take up sailing again. However, until he disappears over the horizon, you can find him at www.mauriceclaypole.com

CONTENTS

Foreword
    by Elke Schulth 9
Some of the questions answered in this book................12
Introduction... 13
Goodbye to all that
    The death of the communicative approach................... 15
The best of both worlds
    Implementing blended learning in ELT 25
Second Life comes of age
    Teaching English in a virtual world 35
The road to Nowhere Land
    Teaching International English 43
More sex please, we're British
    Teaching the language of sex 49
On your bike!
    The secret to being a good English teacher...................56
Why most teachers are sluts
    Do native speakers really make better EFL teachers? ... 61
Myth or magic?
    Technology and parapsychology in ELT 68
Not such a poor relation
    The role of translation in language teaching 75
Context, content, COLT
    How to teach Technical English.......................................85
The circles of your mind
    Introducing word set maps 102
Chaos and dynamism in language teaching
    The birth of the fractal approach 111
Acknowledgments 124

Foreword

'Methodology is... a dynamic, creative, and exploratory process that begins anew each time the teacher encounters a group of learners.' (Richards, 2001)

I will never forget our first email contact on a cold, February day in 2009. Maurice Claypole had congratulated me on my re-election as Chair of ELTAS (English Language Teaching Association Stuttgart). At that time, our teachers' association was engaged in a heated debate about whether to continue issuing our professional journal, *ETM* (*English Teaching Matters*) or move on to the more modern idea of blogging on our website. He seemed to have sensed my need for a more critical view on the matter. He wrote that it had been his policy not to interfere with the work of subsequent committees but would always be ready to provide assistance if required. After all, he had been Chair of ELTAS from 2000 – 2004 and 'knew the ropes', as they say.

During his term of office as Chair of ELTAS, Maurice had set major milestones and laid a solid foundation on which ELTAS could build. He launched the ELTAS website, created its logo and together with his wife Ann, founded *English Teaching Matters*. This professional magazine has become our glossy visiting card for the outside world, as well as for our sister organizations in Hamburg (HELTA), Berlin (ELTAB), Ulm (ELTAU) and Eastern Westphalia-Lippe (ELTA OWL).

On the occasion of our 20th anniversary on 4 July 2009, Maurice graciously accepted our offer to give a speech on the origins and history of ELTAS. He treated his audience to a fascinating insight into the state of ELT (English Language Teaching) at the time ELTAS was founded and made us think of how our profession has dramatically changed since then. His talk was elegantly complemented by our guest speaker David Graddol, applied linguist, broadcaster, researcher, consultant and author of **The Future of English** and **English Next**, who directed our attention to

Global Trends in ELT. This special event will remain as a hallmark in the history of ELTAS.

Maurice remains a regular contributor to *ETM* and ever since the winter of 2007, has published in it a series of particularly controversial articles on English as a Foreign (or Second) Language (EFL/ESL). I am sure that, due to the provocative nature of his columns, they have sparked off many a discussion 'behind the scenes' and encouraged many a teacher to rethink certain topics and to question traditional views.

This book is an enticing collection of such articles. Controversy is evident from the very first chapter, entitled **Goodbye to all that – The death of the communicative approach.**

The communicative approach was a teaching concept born in the 1970's and developed by pioneers such as David Wilkins. At that time, ELT was very grammar-focused. However, Wilkins believed in homing in on the concept of language use and not relying entirely on technicalities of grammar. Teaching how and when to use the language appropriately, combined with spoken as well as written grammar, he argued, was of central importance (Harmer, 2007). Despite diverse reservations, this teaching method has had a great impact on teaching and learning worldwide. Yet Maurice claims this approach has been

> '... so often misunderstood, misinterpreted and misused that it has outlived its usefulness – and worse still, has in some instances become an excuse for poor or inappropriate teaching.'

What could be more controversial?

At this point, I would like to ask Maurice, 'Why have you kept us waiting so long?' It was high time to dust off the cobwebs in the EFL/ELT business. This book provides a refreshing look at old concepts, opens our eyes to new perspectives and encourages teachers to venture along new paths. I wish you, the reader, ever-growing horizons.

Elke Schulth
Chair,
English Language Teachers Association Stuttgart (ELTAS)

References

Harmer, J. (2007) 'Popular Methodology' in Harmer, J. (Ed), *The Practice of English language teaching*, 4th edition, Pearson Education Ltd., p. 69-70

Richards, J. (2001) 'Beyond Methods' in Candlin, C. N. and Mercer, N. (eds.), *English language teaching in its social context: A reader*, Routledge, p. 167 - 179

Some of the questions answered in this book

- Where did communicative language teaching go wrong?
- If the communicative approach is dead, what do I use instead?
- Why did the grammar/translation method fall out of favour?
- Is the language teacher a trainer, facilitator, role model or what?
- Can I teach translation without teaching grammar?
- What is blended learning and how can I exploit it?
- How do I find the time to set up interactive online lessons?
- Are virtual worlds important for language learning?
- Can I teach English in Second Life and why should I?
- Should I teach culture and if so, which?
- Why is the concept of International English misguided?
- Should I talk about sex in the classroom?
- Why is humour important in English language teaching?
- Should there be taboos in the language classroom?
- How can I teach my students intimate language?
- What is the secret of being a good English teacher?
- Can you learn a language from a dictionary?
- Which is better: teacher-centred learning or learner-centred teaching?
- Are native English speakers really better teachers than non-natives?
- Should I use the student's first language in class?
- Is it the teacher's job to promote skills?
- My students want everything translated. What should I do?
- Should I try to make my students think in English?
- How can I use translation as an aid to teaching?
- What makes a good translation?
- How can I teach Technical English more effectively?
- What is the importance of content in language teaching?
- How can I explain how items of vocabulary interact?
- Why don't grammar rules work?
- Are interactive whiteboards an indispensable tool?
- What is Superlearning?
- Do suggestopaedic techniques work?
- What are word set maps and how can I create them?
- Why don't words have fixed meanings?
- What should I be teaching my advanced students?
- How does context affect meaning?
- How do the dynamics of language affect my teaching?
- Why are there no right answers?
- What is the fractal approach to ELT?

Introduction

Most of these papers were originally published in *English Teaching Matters* (ISSN 1862-4626) under the heading 'Controversies in EFL'. Since *ETM* is a quarterly periodical, these columns appeared over a period of two years – from 2007 to 2009. The chapter on blended learning predates the Controversies column but has since become a highly topical (and controversial) issue affecting almost all language teachers. The chapter on the role of translation in ELT was published in the spring 2008 edition of *Business Issues*. The last three chapters on word set maps, teaching Technical English and the fractal approach draw on papers and lectures I have given over the years, but which have never before been made available to a wider audience.

Although little has changed in ELT since the majority of these papers first appeared, awareness of some of the topics covered has certainly increased in the interim. In particular, more and more observers are now questioning the value of the communicative approach, whilst Second Life, unknown to many in the world of ELT when the chapter entitled 'Second Life comes of age' was written, is now firmly established as a platform for language learning.

Other topics, too, have recently achieved much attention, in particular the special skills possessed by teachers of English who are non-native users of the target language.

Although originally intended merely as a somewhat tongue-in-cheek epithet, I feel justified in subtitling this book 'What you always wanted to know about teaching English but were afraid to ask'[1] since the it deals with many topics (e.g. the language of sex,

---

[1] Most readers will recognize the allusion to Dr David Reuben's landmark 1969 book entitled *Everything You Always Wanted to Know About Sex (But Were Afraid to Ask)* and Woody Allen's 1972 movie of the same name.

the values of suggestology, the use of the student's native language as a medium of instruction and the impact on ELT of three-dimensional virtual worlds) which are often omitted from teacher training courses and may in some cases even be regarded as taboo. Some of the questions answered or discussed in varying levels of detail are listed on page 12, but this list is by no means exhaustive.

Because of the deliberately controversial nature of these topics, each paper in this series was introduced in *English Teaching Matters* by the disclaimer that,

'This column is intended to be provocative. Its purpose is to stimulate discussion by presenting a clear point of view, not necessarily all sides of every argument.'

This rider was included in order to grant me a certain amount of journalistic freedom, since space simply did not allow me to present every possible aspect of the topics covered, and this applies equally well to the collection presented here. The content is, however, not as imbalanced as the *ETM* disclaimer might suggest and indeed a great deal of thought and no small amount of research have gone into each of the chapters. But above all, the present book and many of my findings are the result of long years of practical experience.

Only minor changes were made in preparing the original manuscripts for publication, since it seemed right to retain the journalistic style of the articles, which were intended to be both informative and entertaining.

My thanks go to Elke Schulth for contributing the foreword and to my wife Ann for her support in innumerable ways. I would also like to thank all those who have attended my talks and read my columns over the years for encouraging me to put this collection together.

Birkenfeld, February 2010

Goodbye to all that

The death of the communicative approach

A lesson for all concerned

Like so many other things in human history, the communicative approach was born of noble ideas and implemented initially by dedicated specialists. On the basis of its perceived success, it blossomed rapidly, spread throughout the world, taking with it a potential for great good and was widely embraced as the benchmark for modern language teaching. Then it all went pear-shaped.

The communicative approach has run its course.

Let me say at the outset that the communicative approach – or communicative language teaching (CLT) to give it its more accurate alias – is not all bad; some of its basic tenets still apply in some teaching situations. But on the whole it is so often misunderstood, misinterpreted and misused that it has outlived its usefulness – and worse still, has in some instances become an excuse for poor or inappropriate teaching.

The main argument offered in its defence by practitioners of this approach is that it works. Of course it works, for the simple reason that with many types of class and many teaching situations, anything will work. You may be able to knock in a nail with a brick or by tapping it with a rubber hammer, but this does not mean that this is the best way to get the job done. And sometimes a rubber hammer is just not strong enough.

It is not enough to simply claim that a given approach works. There may be other methods which work better.

Let me illustrate this with a personal example:

During a brief stay in China some years ago, I was asked to prepare a couple of private students for the ETS Graduate Record Examinations.[2] This was shortly after the mass rallies were

---

[2] The GRE is taken by prospective graduate applicants and tests verbal reasoning, quantitative reasoning and analytical writing – in other words English and maths. As an example of the level, here is a multiple-choice cloze question from the verbal reasoning section:

15

dispersed in Tian An Men Square, in other words before the opening up of China to mass foreign investment and the widespread expansion of the TEFL market there.

Although they actually majored in other subjects, my students were quite fluent in English, had a good grasp of the mechanics of the language, demonstrated an extensive vocabulary and were willing to learn. Since they were unfamiliar with the Western model of language teaching, they were quite impressed by my communicative methods. My lessons, they said, were so much more interesting and useful than any they had had before. Naturally, I was pleased to have my Western expertise lauded in this way.

Non-communicative methodologies have been used with great success in China.

'So how,' I asked, 'did you learn before?'

'We did exercises,' they replied, and showed me a wad of (not quite legally) photocopied test papers.

'I see,' I said, 'and before that?'

'Our teacher gave us examples,' they replied, 'and explained them in Chinese, so we didn't have the chance to speak English in class.'

In some situations, attitude can be as important a factor as methodology.

'Ah,' I thought to myself proudly, 'this is where I can offer what they have been missing all these years.' Then I said, almost condescendingly, 'But your English is very good. Did you use a book, too?' And at this point, something began to dawn on me. Their English actually was very good. Despite some problems with pronunciation, they were in many ways far more advanced than many of my students back home would be after the same length of study, and they had achieved this with considerably less classroom and media exposure to English. And then they showed me the book they had learnt from. In fact, I already had it – from my initial attempts to grapple with Chinese. It is the little red

---

The actual ------- of Wilson's position was always ------- by his refusal to compromise after having initially agreed to negotiate a settlement.

    (A)   logic...enhanced
    (B)   rigidity...alleviated
    (C)   outcome...foreshadowed
    (D)   cowardice...highlighted

book – not Mao's little red book, but a bilingual pocket dictionary. They had learnt the words – and the pronunciation – from the dictionary. In the absence of native speakers, 'modern' methods and hi-tech aids, they had used the resources they had – to stunning effect. Suddenly, I felt less proud of my methods and more appreciative of the students' determination, commitment and success.

I also realised that although I could now carry out some 'fine tuning' with my communicative methods, I could never have brought them so far in so short a time by focusing on 'communicative' activities. With my tried and tested methods I could easily motivate students and prompt near-beginners to talk; I could promote fluency in elementary and intermediate learners and in the present situation I could put the finishing touches to a high level of achievement. It was the bit in the middle that worried me.

Methodological limitations are more evident at some levels than at others.

What is the communicative approach?

So, just what is the communicative approach anyway? In itself, it is not actually a method of teaching, but a set of assumptions which in turn give rise to a seemingly impressive collection of 'communicative' goals and methodologies.

Put simply, these assumptions are as follows:

- People learn a foreign language in order to communicate.
- Social language functions are an important part of learning a language.
- Classroom activities should reflect the context in which the language is to be used.
- The teacher's main role is to facilitate communication.
- Language acquisition will take place through frequent exposure.
- Fluency is more important to communication than accuracy.

The communicative approach is based on a number of assumptions.

These assumptions generally manifest themselves in classroom practice as follows:

- Students work in groups or in pairs in order to negotiate and transfer meaning.
- Information gaps are crucial to the meaningful transfer of information.
- Authentic materials are used whenever possible.
- Frequent use is made of role-play and simulation.
- Productive skills are emphasised.
- Class work is mainly oral.
- Games, puzzles and quizzes are key classroom techniques.

Implications for the language classroom

These lists are so persuasive and have such a positive aura that it is sometimes difficult to see just how damaging the initial assumptions can be. However, a moment's thought should be enough to call into question the very first assumption – that people learn a foreign language in order to communicate. This may indeed be true in many cases, but in many cases, it is not. There are dozens of other reasons for learning a foreign language, all equally valid, e.g.

Language learning goals are not always communicative.

- to pass an English exam;
- to read scientific or academic papers;
- to understand a foreign culture;
- as an intellectual exercise;
- in order to teach it.

Even many communicative activities are not catered for by current classroom methods.

And even within the communicative paradigm, there are many goals which generally fall outside the scope of the classroom activities listed above, e.g.

- to study a subject through the medium of English

- to write scientific or academic papers
- to reflect mastery of another competence
- to obfuscate, deviate or deflect attention

Furthermore, defining the method according to the goal is in effect putting the cart before the horse. In language learning, there is no objective evidence that learning by doing is better than learning by listening or learning by reading. Practice alone does not make perfect, and encouraging groups of learners to have lively discussions in increasingly fluent broken English can quite simply do more harm than good. It can be like a group of students learning to play the piano by hitting the keys until it comes right.

Practice alone does not make perfect.

Not only are the methods of communicative language teaching not always appropriate, they are not always implementable and in recent years, learners, teachers and institutions in many parts of the world have been finding that communicative methodologies simply do not match their needs. Here are some of the reasons for which the approach may be rejected:

- It is heavily biased towards teachers who are native speakers of English.
- It makes cultural assumptions about the role of the teacher.
- It makes assumptions about the student's mindset and attitude to learning.
- It is hard to implement with very large classes.
- In emphasising language functions, it largely ignores problems of specific content.
- It does not promote accuracy in situations where accuracy is essential.
- It does not provide students with adequate knowledge about the language.

There are many reasons for rejecting communicative language teaching.

Taking the last point, for example, there are many countries in which a learner of English may be expected to go on and teach it. Now, whilst a formal knowledge of structures may not be required to book a hotel room or buy a train ticket, you would expect a teacher of English to have a deeper grasp of the subject matter in order to be able to make informed decisions and selections involving and beyond what his or her students are confronted with in class. After all, who would you prefer to have as a dancing instructor – a talented amateur who had picked up various moves over the years by going with the flow on the dance floor or someone who had learned to break down complex sequences into easy-to-learn steps?

Additional skills and knowledge are required to teach a language.

Why is CLT so persistent?

The communicative credo grew out of a progression of theories and practical experiments, many of which were on shaky ground to start with. Grammar/translation, the direct method (Berlitz), behaviourist audio-lingualism (Skinner) and total physical response (Asher) were only partially supplanted by PPP, functional-notional learning programs and unproven theories relating to the nature of second-language acquisition (Krashen). And whilst linguists were grappling with the notions of systemic functional grammar (Halliday) and generative grammar (Chomsky), classroom practice was neatly sidestepping the issue of formalised language analysis in favour of peer-group teaching and learning by doing something else. Largely compatible with the communicative paradigm are the concepts of task-based learning (Willis), community language learning and the Lexical approach (Lewis), but nothing seems to hang in there with a vengeance in quite the same way as the 'C' word.

The origins of the approach

A methodology based on unproven theories

There are a number of reasons for this:

Why the communicative approach is popular...

- It is popular with students because they are not required to learn formalised grammar, which they assume to be difficult and uninteresting.
- It is popular with teachers because their role as facilitator offers great scope for a wide variety of interesting and fun things to do in the classroom.

- It is popular with publishers because it favours monolingual materials and methods which can be marketed worldwide.

- It is popular with private language schools because there are fewer quantifiable benchmarks and learning becomes an open-ended process.

- It is popular with teacher training organisations because teachers (mainly native speakers of English) can quickly be equipped with a set of skills to get them started in classroom practice.

It is harmful for all the same reasons. Grammar, like any other subject, is only unpopular if it is taught badly, an issue which is not addressed but avoided, churning out second language speakers with little formal knowledge of the target language who have never mastered key language functions such as translation, crafted writing or precise use of structure and meaning. In concentrating on the big picture, the detail gets lost at best, and at worst the result is a stylised form of street English.

... but harmful.

In the sense that the communicative approach works, it works best at certain levels and in certain situations:

- General English
- Small classes
- Native-speaker teachers
- Mid-range learner levels (CEFR A2 – B2)[3]

It works in cases when almost any method will work...

Given these parameters, almost any method will work, in the same way that typing with two fingers works, once you know where the keys are and provided that you are not particularly ambitious.

---

[3] In Europe at least, The *Common European Framework of Reference for Languages: Learning, Teaching Assessment* (CEFR) is rapidly becoming the standard set of benchmarks for describing levels of language proficiency, rendering unnecessary the use of such vague terms as 'elementary', 'intermediate' and 'advanced'.

Outside these parameters, it fails miserably. Publishers are hard-pressed to produce communicative course books for real beginners, and pre-elementary 'starter packs' tend to revert to a grammar-based syllabus incorporating a bilingual element (word lists, translation of rubrics, etc.). Similarly, the method clearly runs out of steam at higher levels. After all, when did you last progress to Book Three of any course package? Furthermore, it does not work once you introduce specific content.

... but not for real beginners or at higher levels.

The importance of content

The question of content is crucial here, since **what** you teach is far more important than **how** you teach it. Here's another story – this time from my experience of teaching English in Germany: some time ago I had cause to call in on my local adult education institute just as registrations for the forthcoming term's evening courses were getting under way. A migrant worker from Eastern Europe was trying to sign up for an intermediate German course.

The course content should reflect the students' needs.

'I'm sorry,' said the receptionist, 'but that course is full. Would you like to do French instead?' You laugh. Wait.

A former freelance colleague of mine (let's call her Helga – not her real name) was asked by an engineering company to teach Technical English. The company manufactures swaging machines and roller mills. Not knowing anything about swaging machines and not being able to find any relevant lesson material in any of the course books she possessed, Helga concluded that what the students really needed to do was communicate with customers and business partners, so she taught them to hold meetings, make phone calls and write emails, leaving the technical content to the students. After all, she wasn't expected to know anything about swaging machines, was she? She was an English teacher, not an engineer. Since the students were in fact quite good at making phone calls and writing emails, it was just a matter of fine-tuning their skills and so the course 'went well' and Helga was satisfied. The students never complained and Helga got paid. Funnily, though, the company did not renew her contract.

The attitude of the teacher is crucial.

Part of the problem is not the approach itself, but the teacher's attitude to the approach. On one occasion, I was teaching an in-company Business English course as part of a team – a team put together by the client. Another teacher and myself had been engaged to teach one week each of a two-week intensive course culminating in a preset mini-exam. We had never worked together before; in fact we had never met – not a problem in itself, of course, because we were both experienced freelancers; we simply needed to agree upon who would do what. What took me aback a little, however, was the other teacher's introductory suggestion:

'I have them for the first week, so I'll do the communicative bit, then you can just go in and teach them the grammar and stuff to get them through the exam.'

A revealing anecdote

To his mind, he would do the 'real' teaching using 'modern' methods to 'get them talking', maybe bring in a newspaper or a video, do some role play and maybe practice a few phone calls, then in the second week I could help them cram for the exam using boring old-fashioned methods like structured exercises, detailed error correction and so on, and actually get them to write something.

Just to test the water, I said, 'OK, but why don't we do it the other way round, with you doing the grammar in the first week? After all, they'll be able to communicate much better once they have a solid base of grammar and vocabulary.'

There was a long pause. Then to his credit he came clean: he had been teaching for a long time, but he didn't actually know much formal grammar and always skipped the 'boring bits' in the course books. He just didn't feel too comfortable, he said, where exams were involved, because exams test old-fashioned stuff like verbs, word-order and spelling.

Clearly, the majority of his other courses were of a more general nature for which communicative methods were better suited. Learning could take place over a suitably long period of time and everybody would have fun in the process. But short-term goals such as exams punched a hole right through his methods.

The approach must match the content.

The approach needs to fit the content, not vice versa. In Business English classes you can just about get away with it because a lot of general English is used in business, but enter the domain of true ESP and teachers of the communicative school find that their methods simply do not work any more.

Expectations have changed. As an umbrella concept for a set of teaching methods, the approach has run its course because it was based on false assumptions in the first place, and because student expectations in terms of form and content have changed. Never embraced in quite the same way in state schools or for languages other than English, it has led inevitably to questionable classroom practice and low levels of student competency in key areas of writing, translating and critical reading.

Getting results is more important than the choice of approach. Behaviourist reinforcement also works on the teacher: positive feedback from students who are enjoying the lesson because they don't have to 'work' will naturally encourage the teacher to continue in the same vein, often blissfully unaware that in terms of learning, better results could be attained by other methods, a matter which the students themselves are in no position to judge and which does not unduly concern the teacher in the heat of the moment. In consequence, the approach has left us with a generation of teachers around the world who spend an undue amount of time flapping their arms around and drawing unnecessary sketches to explain abstract concepts when they could simply slip into the students' own language and get the job done much faster and more effectively. The communicative approach is easy on the teacher and fun for the learner but ultimately slow and counter-productive.

If it works – use it! What should you do instead? Well, a number of suggestions will be made in subsequent chapters, but to put it in a nutshell: redefine your goals and choose the method that fits the job in hand. I started my excursion by reminiscing about a trip to China, so I will close with a comment attributed to the Chinese leader at that time, Deng Xiaoping: 'It doesn't matter if a cat is black or white, as long as it catches mice.'

The best of both worlds
Implementing blended learning in ELT

There has been a great deal of media hype about blended learning and my impression is that many English teachers would be prepared to implement its techniques if only they knew what was involved, whereas others may see blended learning as yet another example of unwelcome technology invading the classroom. I will therefore try to define blended learning, outline the benefits it can bring to both teacher and student and show how the principles involved can be implemented in English language teaching.

How teachers respond to blended learning

Let me begin by saying what blended learning is not. It is **not** the same as computer-based training (CBT) or web-based training (WBT), although these may be important components. Nevertheless it is closely associated with computers and the internet. My own involvement in computer-assisted learning started in the early 1980's. In fact I wrote my first EFL programs in PASCAL in 1979, working on university mainframes and progressed to home computers and personal computers as the technology appeared. However, the technology never really lived up to expectations, so when I completed my PhD thesis on artificial intelligence in computer-assisted EFL self-study techniques in 1990, I closed the book on the subject. For a decade, that is. By 2000, advances in technology, and particularly in internet connectivity, meant that the time was ripe to introduce a new element into courses that we were developing at my language school (LinguaServe) – and this more integrated approach has recently become known as blended learning.

Origins of computer-assisted learning

In theory, it should be a fairly easy matter to define blended learning; however, there would seem to be as many definitions as there are commentators. In general, we can identify four different concepts to which it can refer:

So what is blended learning?

1. A combination of different pedagogical approaches such as behaviouristic, holistic, cognitive, communicative, etc.
2. A combination of instructional technology and work-based tasks within a corporate learning program
3. A combination of different web-based technologies such as virtual classrooms, streaming video and online learning
4. A combination of any form of instructional technology (e.g. video, DVD/CD-ROM, web-based training, broadcast media) and face-to-face teaching

Blended learning therefore means different things to different people and covers the whole spectrum of education and training, much of which is not relevant to teaching EFL, so I will restrict myself here to the methods that we have actually implemented at my school and to describing what can be achieved in the short term by EFL teachers working with limited resources.

From this point of view, I would like to define blended learning as follows:

Working definition of blended learning

The integrated use of human and electronic delivery platforms and communication techniques, tailored or adapted to suit the needs of the learner and the capabilities of the teacher

Nowadays, most adult learners use email for distance communication and for many the internet is a prime source of information, but in only a very few cases has their experience of computer-based training or online learning been truly successful. Despite the move towards e-learning and i-learning in recent years, classroom training is still the norm for all types and levels of English. One reason for this is that the classroom provides a social experience and promotes direct language interaction, whereas e-learning can be a solitary activity requiring a great deal of discipline on the part of the student and also lacks the immediacy and flexibility of the classroom. It is not realistic in the short term to replace classroom teaching with a technology-based learning solution, but it is possible to combine classroom teaching with appropriate forms of electronic delivery to give teacher and student the best of both worlds. But simply adopting a standard software package, however good it may be in itself, and including it in the course concept, whether as part of the classroom activity or as a homework component, does not in my view represent a blending of resources. A standard software solution is in essence an electronic course book; its contents are predefined and its authors do not know precisely who the students are. A solution is therefore needed that, like any good teacher, puts the needs of the students first and which allows control of content and delivery to remain with the teacher.

Combining face-to-face classroom activities with appropriate electronic self-study

In other words, I believe that effective blended learning in English language teaching should be **learner-centred but teacher-driven.**

Learner-centred, but teacher-driven

It must be learner-centred because losing sight of the learner is the cardinal sin of all bad teaching, whilst learner awareness the hallmark of all good teaching; and it should be teacher-driven because in ELT the teacher still provides the language model. He or she should be empowered to deliver or to guide the online component as well as the face-to-face element of a blended learning course.

At LinguaServe we have worked on a number of blended learning projects over the years and have gradually developed a technique which replaces static learnware by a series of task-based exercises requiring the students to use the internet as a source of information and language study. These tasks are then integrated into the face-to-face seminars and supported by a variety of print materials and specifically customised software. The students are prepared for the online phase by carrying out their first tasks under supervision during the seminar phase.

From static software to task-based internet study

27

Implementing blended learning for a major trade union

Additional interactive exercises are created by the teachers and delivered to the students via the internet during the self-study phase. These exercises complement the internet-based research tasks and indeed are so constructed that they provide further consolidation of the vocabulary and language learned.

Range of tasks and exercise types

As a basis for the electronic component, we use eight different exercise types, ranging from multiple choice and short answer quizzes to sentence jumbles, crosswords and drag-and-drop exercises. Each task can either stand alone or be accompanied by a reading text or similar input. The following example shows a multiple-choice quiz based on a reading text, which in turn is based on a news item the students had discussed in class.

CONTROVERSIES IN ELT

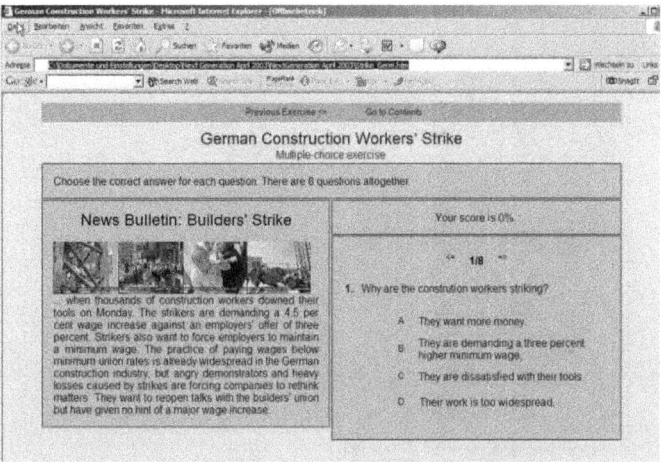

Illustrated text with multiple-choice tasks

The reading text can be revealed when the program is run, masked at first and revealed later or displayed for a limited time only. The student can be offered help or hints as deemed necessary in each individual case. But because he or she is actually working online, the learner can also call up online dictionaries or reference works whilst solving the tasks. In fact, links to other internet sites can be added to the program to provide the student with a real-time online source of information. In other words, the program as delivered is also a link to the outside world, ensuring that its content always automatically up-to-date.

Teacher and resources online

In a further extension, sound and video can be added, enabling comprehension activities to be incorporated into the online learning phase. And because the multimedia files are created in a standard data format, they can be read by whatever application the user has installed. There is no danger of a custom output system colliding with the memory management of the user's machine. In fact, anything that is available as a PC or internet-compatible file can be incorporated into the online lesson. In the variation below, clicking on the link in the right-hand half of the

Universal standard format

29

screen launches the video sequence in the student's own application.

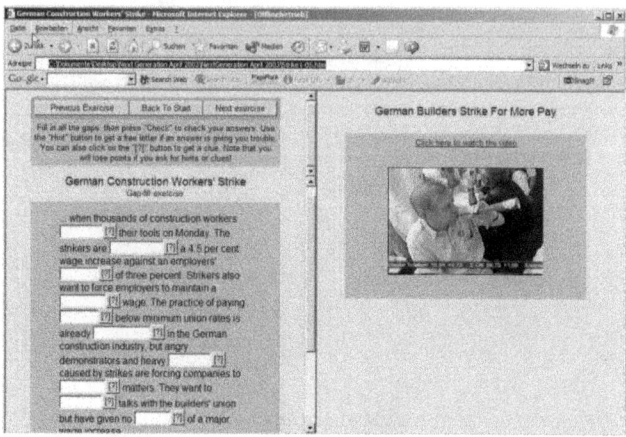

Integrated cloze exercise and video input

Online support from face-to-face teacher

These activities are backed up by email support from the same teacher who is running the face-to-face seminars, and each exercise can easily and quickly be tailored to the needs and language level of the particular target group.

The examples shown above are taken from the self-study phase of an intensive industry-specific course in which several weeks separate each seminar block of three or four consecutive days. In these courses, we use a wide variety of additional techniques, including a discussion forum, case studies, simulation, live video and a variety of team teaching methods (see *English Teaching Matters* Vol. 3 No. 3 September 2002), but the electronic component can also be applied to short courses or regular, once-a-week classes.

Spontaneous and flexible online activities

The real beauty of blended learning is the flexibility provided by modern authoring systems, which enable the teacher to create online homework activities spontaneously from lesson to lesson. The examples below were created ad-hoc shortly after a lesson with a hybrid (part Business English part General English) course and fulfil a number of different functions.

The start-up page consists of a digital snapshot of the whiteboard taken immediately after the lesson; it shows some of the words used during the unscripted warm-up phase of the lesson. These words are then incorporated into a web-based quiz (not shown here) and followed by a crossword highlighting the key vocabulary from the main lesson content. Finally, a new task is set which requires the students to locate some specific information on the internet and report their findings back to the teacher by email before the next lesson.

Extending unscripted classroom material into the web-based experience

These pages are made available to the students via the internet a few days after their weekly lesson, providing both a specifically-targeted revision exercise and a starting point for the following week's lesson.

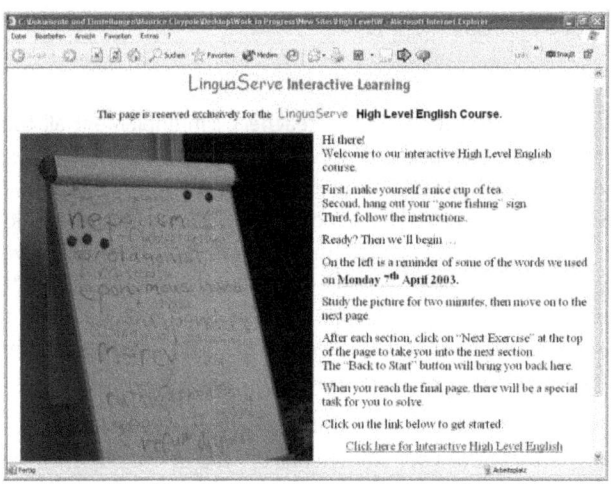

Impromptu web lesson based the on classroom experience

CONTROVERSIES IN ELT

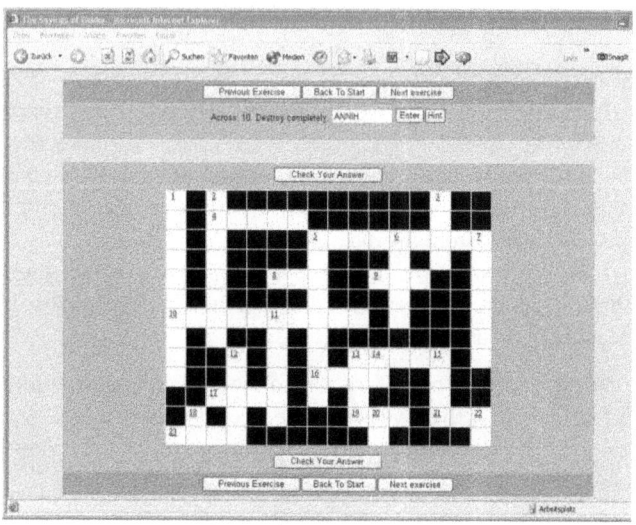

Customised online crossword (also printable)

How to get started

I am not suggesting that all teachers can implement all these techniques immediately, or that they are suitable for all courses, but if you would like to experiment, you will probably start with just one or two techniques and courses. Let's consider this idea in its simplest form. It could mean a transition from telling your students, 'have a look at page 97 for homework' to saying, 'For your homework, look in your mailbox on Tuesday and do the tasks you will find there' or 'Do the tasks on page 97 and email your answers to me by Wednesday.'

Time management is important.

At this point you may well object that you don't have time to write letters to all your students or to read all the pieces of work that might come in by email. My answer to this is that is that you just do what you have time for. Let's say, for example, you set a task via email. Simply setting the task should not take longer than about five minutes, but it could represent an hour's work for the student. And maybe at the end of the tasks, having worked through a series of exercises, there is one question or one solution that they send back to you that indicates that they have actually completed the tasks. In many cases, you don't even have to read the mails, just to acknowledge that so-and-so has done his homework this week and so-and-so has not. The benefit for the students is that they are now getting two lessons a week for the price of one, but you, the teacher, are not actually doing any more work, since the time you invest is deductible from the preparation time you would invest anyway. This represents not only a pedagogical advantage, but also a marketing advantage, especially in the business world where you are selling your services direct to corporate clients.

Let us therefore summarise what blended learning can do for you:

Blended learning

- expands your portfolio of teaching techniques;
- brings your methodology up to date;
- enhances your effectiveness as a teacher;   *Benefits for the teacher*
- accelerates learning;
- increases your marketability;
- provides added customer satisfaction;
- creates a more rounded teaching/learning experience;
- positions you for the next technological leap - whatever that might be.

However, I would advise strongly against trying to jump on a perceived bandwagon by buying a set of CBT or WBT tools and creating courses for which you hope to attract students or even advertising courses that you hope to be able to create once the students register. What I would advise is to expand the methods you currently use on your existing courses to incorporate an element of e-learning or internet-based task work. It will then

Incorporate e-learning into your existing classes.

Blended learning is not about technology.

follow automatically that you offer similar components to new courses, students or business clients. The extent and form of this implementation depends on you, the teacher.

Essentially, blended learning is not about technology; it is about creativity.

Related links

http://www.blended-learning-in-elt.com

http://www.linguaserve.biz/tui

http://www.linguaserve-online.com

Second Life comes of age
Teaching English in a virtual world

From today, Moodle is dead. Virtual learning environments (VLEs) as we know them are a thing of the past. Goodbye Skype. Adieu Quia, Telos and Flash animation. Second Life has arrived.

But before I proceed further, let me put this claim in context. At our language school, we have been delivering blended learning courses since the year 2000. While the technology has changed a lot since then, the basic methodologies have not. On the technical side, our first corporate blended learning contract not only required custom software but also involved loaning a Macintosh laptop to each student and setting up a dedicated server to handle email traffic. Although we were using client-specified technology and were not actually responsible for the technical aspects, much of our time as teachers was spent dealing with software and data transfer issues. When we subsequently developed our own software solutions, we endeavoured to use freely available and readily understood technology so that it would not be intrusive, and in our 2003 Blended Learning lecture tour and article of the same year, I emphasised that blended learning 'is not about technology, it is about creativity' and that one of the key advantages for the English teacher is that involvement 'positions you for the next technological leap – whatever that might be.'[4] I believe that the time is now ripe to make that leap and to reappraise and redefine our current notions of virtual learning environments and blended learning systems.

The early days of blended learning

The next technological leap

Consider the following: a student – let's call her Sophie – spends part of her course time meeting face-to-face with other students and her teacher, Dan. They practice pronunciation and speaking, do some written work and interact in any number of ways.

A language school where virtually anything is possible...

---

[4] See previous chapter and *English Teaching Matters* Vol. 4 No. 3

... from classroom study and homework...

Following the face-to-face lesson, Sophie does follow-up homework via the school's web site and submits her work to her tutor for discussion at the next meeting. Since part of her course is based on a standard published EFL book, she also uses print and audio material offline. Occasionally, she watches a course video at home and completes the accompanying self-learning exercises, checking her answers against the key.

.. to student social life...

Before her next scheduled lesson, Sophie meets up with other students to discuss the course and to practice what they have learned. They chat about other matters, too, and find common interests outside the classroom. Sophie and two of her classmates, Raoul and Studebaker, take a balloon ride and go skydiving together.

... and study trips.

Occasionally, the class takes a field trip to look at some cultural issues. On a trip to Dublin they visit Trinity College, where Dan studied to be a teacher and he tells them about his student days there and shows them around the building. Then they move on to an Irish bar, the Blarney Stone, to hear some folk music and mix with the regulars. On another occasion, they fly to London to travel on the tube, do some shopping in Knightsbridge and call in at the Underground Club. Talin Silverstar, their favourite DJ, is spinning discs for a dozen or so groovy ravers and then it's time for a trivia quiz at the Three Bells with cash prizes for the first correct answer to each question.

Meanwhile, another group of students, together with their teacher, Brianny, are taking in some culture of a different kind by attending a performance of Shakespeare's *Hamlet* at the Globe Theatre.

Back in class, the students meet to compare their experiences and discuss their trips while the teachers deal with any language issues that arise. At an appropriate point, they move on to the next lesson in the scheduled programme.

Is this blended learning? You bet it is. And no less so because the 'face-to-face' meetings and class outings took place in Second Life. Do any of the people involved ever meet 'face-to-face' in the 'real world'? Well, that would be difficult, because Sophie is in

Stuttgart and Dan is in Tokyo. And her classmates are not just from São Paulo, Oslo and New Delhi. They are still there. All these events are taking place in a three-dimensional virtual environment called Second Life.

It has taken blended learning a long time to become a household word and we are already on the verge of the next big leap sideways – a paradigm shuffle of the highest order. In Star Trek, Mr Spock reportedly commented on some new species of intergalactic oofle dust, 'It's life, Jim, but not as we know it'[5] and the same applies in many ways to Second Life. Familiar things exist but they exist in a different way.

The future of blended learning?

Second Life

Second Life is a virtual world inhabited by real people who live, work and play in an environment they have created themselves. It is both a game and a serious application; it is both ordered and anarchic. It is a three-dimensional metaverse in which – within certain social, moral and legal constraints – you can look and act as you please. And in the short term at least, it is the future of online learning.

Second Life is a community run by real people...

The London Borough of Knightsbridge recreated in Second Life

---

[5] This is the version that has entered popular culture but is in fact a misquotation of what Leonard Nimoy actually said, which was: 'No life as we know it.' (Season 1 Episode 25: *The Devil in the Dark* (1967))

There are a lot of things that you can do in Second Life that have no direct relevance to language teaching – build a house, start a business, go shopping, dancing, surfing and swimming, drive a car, pilot a plane, sail a boat, use firearms, make friends, etc. In a way, these activities simply mirror the real world in which we teach, and the fact that these things are going on elsewhere at the same time, does not stop us teaching English. On the contrary, it provides an environment in which we can teach more effectively. And of course there are some things you can do easily in Second Life which knock the virtual stuffing out of the real world – you can grow wings and fly, teleport instantly to another location, walk underwater, etc.

... with everything that life within a community entails.

Against this background, regular class work may sound rather boring, but here are just a few things you can do in this 3D environment that are directly relevant to ELT:

In Second Life, ELT relevant aspects abound.

- Form groups and communities
- Administer courses
- Hold classes, discussions and meetings
- Engage in role play
- Carry out case studies
- Set and monitor tasks
- Give presentations
- Distribute handouts
- Exchange text messages
- Speak and listen to others
- Create exercises
- Organise field trips
- Set homework
- Check homework
- Organise conferences
- Advertise services
- Socialise

As I write, many people seem to be heavily influenced by the notion that Second Life is a game and therefore not to be taken seriously, and it is certainly true that this microcosm of society and its technology were originally developed as a gaming platform. But it has grown into something much bigger and is being taken very seriously in the business world. Most big-name corporations have an inworld (Second Life) operation and this includes not just techies such as Microsoft and IBM but also, for example, sportswear maker Nike and fashion retailer H & M. In addition, this virtual environment is rapidly being developed as a platform for cultural and educational events.

The business world is moving into Second Life.

A meeting of educators at SL Languages

In 2010, Second Life currently has some 18 million registered users and of these between 40,000 and 60,000 are online at any one time, so the scope of organisations represented is correspondingly vast. Harvard University has a considerable presence there, as do hundreds of other colleges and universities. Numerous virtual pop concerts are held every day and in September 2007 the Royal Liverpool Philharmonic Orchestra performed for the first time in its own Virtual Philharmonic Hall. In October of the same year the UK's first ever Virtual World Careers Fair was held in Second Life. Due to the number of applicants, they had to go through a screening process, with some 80 candidates being shortlisted to participate. Most major political parties and many charitable associations have virtual offices in Second Life.

Colleges and universities are major users.

Second Life has been running since 2003 but in my view only came of age on August 2nd 2007 when voice was introduced. It is the combination of easy-to-use computer animation and voice capability that sets it apart from all other learning platforms and

Second Life became of interest to ELT when voice facilities were introduced.

makes it virtually predestined for distance-based language teaching.

Teaching English in Second Life

Although at least one language learning conference has taken place within Second Life[6], the teaching of English inworld is still very much in its infancy. As far as I can tell, LinguaServe is the first real world language school with a parallel existence in Second Life, i.e. trading under the same name and providing comparable services in both worlds, but there are currently three or four other inworld organisations offering or preparing to offer English classes, most prominently Languagelab, SL English, Avatar English, Drive-Through ESL and SL Languages.[7]

Why maintain a learning platform in Second Life?

There are a number of reasons for establishing a learning platform in Second Life. It is not the only 3D environment available to language teachers, but no other can currently compete with its breadth and sophistication. Like the internet, people are already using it for other purposes, a fact which promotes growth and enhances acceptability. Basic membership is free and there is just one piece of software to install. You do not even need a web browser. Also, like the internet, once users have familiarised themselves with the system, the technology is not intrusive. On the contrary, it can be fun.

Virtual performances take place at the New SL Globe Theatre.

---

[6] The Second Life Conference on Learning Foreign Languages, held on 23 June 2007 at EduNation. See the web site of the hosts: http://www.theconsultants-e.com.

[7] These groups can easily be located inworld by using the inworld Search function.

If you want to know more, the premier source of general information is the Second Life website[8], whilst information on teaching English inworld can be obtained from Second Life ELT[9].

How to get started in Second Life

Discussion corner of a virtual classroom

Due to the recent introduction of the voice facility and other technical changes, most books on the subject, including the much-heralded official guide to Second Life (Wiley Publishing Inc., 2007) are already way out of date.

In conclusion, I believe that my 2003 definition of blended learning as 'the integrated use of human and electronic delivery platforms and communication techniques, tailored or adapted to suit the needs of the learner and the capabilities of the teacher' still holds true, but communication techniques have changed so

---

[8] The metaverse's official website is run by its creators, Linden Labs at http://www.secondlife.com.
[9] Second Life ELT is currently being developed as a free resource for teachers: http://www.secondlife-elt.com.

radically that in many areas the process of tailoring and adapting has only just begun. The future belongs not to Moodles, but to Sloodles[10].

The author's virtual persona...   *... modelled on the real thing*

---

[10] Sloodle stands for Second Life Object-Oriented Distributed Learning Environment. See http://www.sloodle.org.

The road to Nowhere Land

Teaching International English

It is over forty years since John Lennon penned the words:

> *He's a real nowhere man*
>
> *Living in his nowhere land*
>
> *Making all his nowhere plans*
>
> *For nobody*[11]

and yet he could have been writing about the state of ELT in the twenty-first century.

Rather than teaching the English of any particular place, many members of the profession are now teaching the English of Nowhere Land.

The English of Nowhere Land

In response to the innocent query, 'do you teach British or American English?', it is not unusual for teachers and institutions to point out that of the world's one and a half billion or so speakers of English, many come from neither the UK nor the USA and that what the students are expected to learn is a universal form of 'International English' which will equip them for travel to or dealings with any English-speaking country.

Whilst the goals and sentiment behind this response may indeed be noble and well-meaning, this reply not only totally

---

[11] Nowhere Man (© Northern Songs) was first released in 1966 on the album *Rubber Soul* in the UK and on *"Yesterday" ...and Today* in the USA. It was credited to Lennon/McCartney as a matter of course, but is clearly a John Lennon song. It was also used in the 1968 movie *Yellow Submarine*. For rare footage of the band performing the song live at the Circus Krone in Munich go to http://www.youtube.com/watch?v=yRv34Cat3Vw.

misses the point, it is highly patronising and ultimately untrue. A little thought will reveal that the enquirer is probably aware of the existence of such places as Canada, Australia, New Zealand and South Africa and of the fact that English is spoken in these countries, but they also know which cultures and language variants exert the most influence over their particular sphere of interest. In short, there is a sound reason behind their seemingly ingenuous question. The potential student expects to be taught a language within a specific context and may even have a preference in the matter. But in striving to teach some form of generic International English, the language provider is studiously ignoring this key customer requirement.

Everybody comes from somewhere.

It is revealing that one of the first questions we ask a new acquaintance is, 'Where are you from?' Why do we ask this? Because in many cases, it is the single most useful thing to know about a person. After all, **everybody comes from somewhere.** However, much recent emphasis on various forms of international or standardised English and the tendency to design courses and publish course books with a global perspective at the cost of any one particular orientation give the impression that it's somehow undesirable to teach English with a specific cultural, ethnic or geographical focus in mind. Teaching British English or American English (or any other variety) is out of fashion to the point of becoming a big no-no.

Doesn't have a point of view
Knows not where he's going to

International English will not help your students.

Teaching a generalised form of International English, however, will always put your students at a disadvantage. International English is the culture of nowhere and in a world of somewhere people, speakers of International EFL will always be understood, but will never fully understand their counterparts. In short, a native speaker may well understand everything the students say, but there will be an unnecessarily large deficit in the opposite direction.

*He's as blind as he can be
Just sees what he wants to see*

Of course, there is nothing wrong with International English, Globish, Basic English and so on if all a learner wants to do is book a railway ticket and find their hotel. But in fact, **any form of English will prepare them for these tasks.** Once they reach the Intermediate (CEFR B1) stage they really should be aiming higher. And that does not mean learning more grammar; it means learning to use language in a real world context by empathising with people who come from somewhere. The language of an educated native speaker is rich in allusion, innuendo and shared inferences drawn from the worlds of entertainment, sport, current affairs and above all national television.

At higher levels, real-world content is needed.

In a contextual sense, students who learn only a generalised form of English inevitably find themselves hopelessly out of their depth when talking to native speakers of any origin.

Nowhere man, can you see me at all?

Indeed, this can even happen to native speakers who find themselves out of context. I witnessed a good example of this recently on the BBC comedy quiz show *QI* chaired by Stephen Fry. The panellists were, if my memory serves me right, Alan Davis (as always) Jo Brandt, Julian Carey and American comedian and writer, Rich Hall. Now, Rich Hall is no dunce and came to prominence with his books about 'sniglets' – words that don't appear in the dictionary but should – but after about 15 minutes of questions and banter about various (British) TV shows – starting with a translation of Clanger whistling into English and ranging across a wealth of other media references, during which Rich spoke not a word, he had to admit that his silence was due to the fact that he 'hadn't understood anything since the Clangers.' Not being able to draw from the common ground shared by the British panellists, he was exceptionally at a loss for anything to say. In this example, it is only fair to add that the

Even native speakers cannot communicate without a context.

45

position would probably be reversed if a lone British citizen were to find themselves in a room full of people gushing about, let's say, Mork and Mindy or The Brady Bunch.

Knowledge of just one world is better than knowledge of no world at all.

The poor speaker of International English, however, would be equally lost in both worlds. A wise alternative for the teacher, therefore, is to choose a specific target culture and then teach the vernacular, background and mores of that target area in greater depth.

Isn't he a bit like you and me?

Teach the type of English the students need — even if you are not a native speaker of it.

So which cultural variant of English should a teacher focus on? Clearly, a lot will depend on who you are, who your students are and how much control you have over the syllabus. As a native of the USA, for instance, you will clearly be in a better position to give first-hand knowledge of American rather than British usage, idiom and custom, but if your students have a particular interest in the UK, whether for reasons of travel, business, culture or on the simple basis of proximity, then you may need to shift the emphasis and even do some background research yourself, otherwise you may not be equipping your students with the language skills they need. Of course, the same principle applies if you are British but your students' main focus is the USA or in the case of any other combination of origins and target cultures.

International English is non-standard English.

As speakers of a second language, students can never be expected to master the language of the entire world any more than a native speaker can, but unlike a native speaker, the speakers of International English or Globish in its various manifestations have learnt a soulless, rootless form of English which will only work because everyone they meet will instinctively talk down to them, a fact of which the learners are often blissfully unaware. Of course, they may realise that they can not follow a conversation between native speakers, but frequently assume that this is because the locals are using some form of dialect or slang, whereas in a way, quite the reverse is true. It is the Globish itself that is a non-standard form of English.

CONTROVERSIES IN ELT

Nowhere man, please listen,
You don't know what you're missin'

It is with a wry smile that I recall a three-way conversation I once had in a little place called Ron's Bar in downtown San Francisco. I was chatting to the barman about baseball (the rumour at the time was that the Giants were about to be sold) when a tall, thirsty backpacker breezed in, took the bar stool next to mine and gestured his order for a beer. I was in need of a refill too, and as the barman went over to the tap, picking up a few more orders on the way, I engaged in pleasantries with the newcomer, who introduced himself as Dave. It quickly transpired that he was Australian, and since Oz had been having a good day in the field, the conversation naturally turned to cricket. When the barman came back with the drinks, he assumed that we were still on baseball, so we picked up our previous conversation while Dave was initially unaware that the topic had even changed until the barman asked him for his take on the LA Dodgers. Dave had clearly not been in town long, but he was far from stupid and made some general comments about the game of baseball. It didn't help. Dave's vowel sounds were as much a mystery to the Californian barman as the Dodgers and Giants were to Dave, and at that point it struck me that while I could chat easily with the barman about baseball and with Dave about cricket, they could hardly carry on a conversation with each other. Of course, I realise that at another time and place our roles could easily be switched and I might be the one left gawping in incomprehension; but a speaker of generic International English would be at a loss almost everywhere.

There was an American, an Australian and an Englishman...

.. but travel and awareness are more important than nationality.

Nowhere Man, don't worry,
Take your time, don't hurry,
Leave it all till somebody else
Lends you a hand

Another area where current notions of International English can go awry is the tendency to interpret the 'inter' as meaning

'Inter' means between the students' culture and that of their target community.

between the English-speaking world and the rest, whereas ideally it should be between the students' culture and that of their main language focus, which may be the UK, the USA or somewhere else entirely, but not the language of Nowhere Land.

Indeed, there is so much variety within the English-speaking world that no internationally-oriented book or course can cover more than a limited and carefully selected range of material, and in practice there is a real danger of teachers and course book authors resorting to second-hand knowledge, half-truths and banalities about countries they have never even visited, whereas they frequently have at their disposal a wealth of in-depth first-hand knowledge of their own culture which is sadly being suppressed on the grounds that it is too specific or too parochial.

Meaningful language learning demands focus and content.

The danger of too much internationalism is not only a loss of identity; it is a loss of ability. Language can not be mastered in vague terms; meaningful learning requires focus and context. In essence, there is no such thing as International English, nor any need to create it.

Teach someone to speak British or American English well, and they'll cope anywhere in the world.

Nowhere man, the world is at your command

Or at least it should be.

More sex please, we're British

Teaching the language of sex

Most readers will probably recognise the indirect allusion in the title of this chapter; the partially eponymous farce *No Sex Please, We're British* by Alistair Foot and Anthony Marriott was one of the longest-running West End comedies ever, playing to packed houses for most of the nineteen-seventies. The subject of the play is, of course, the archetypal British reserve and aloofness in all matters sexual, and the plot turns around the plight of newly-wed assistant bank manager Peter Hunter, played when I saw the show at the Strand Theatre in 1975 by Andrew Sachs[12] just before he rose to fame as hapless Spanish waiter Manuel in *Fawlty Towers*. In the stage play, Hunter unwittingly becomes the recipient of a flood of adult material and not surprisingly, mayhem ensues as he attempts to conceal it from all those around him. Under the rules of traditional British values as they are frequently lampooned on stage and screen, sex is not something to be paraded on paper or discussed in the home. Or, for that matter, in the ELT classroom.

Traditional British attitudes to sex

Elsewhere in this book, we shall look at some of the various roles that EFL/ESL teachers may need to play, such as that of mentor, facilitator, role model, language resource, etc. but one of the key roles that is seldom discussed in ELT studies is that of gap-filler. For various reasons, most teachers find themselves using course books or some other prescribed or pre-defined teaching material for the majority of their classes, since the alternative would largely involve re-inventing the wheel. However, few course books are a perfect match for every class within their target group, so good teachers do their best to fill in the gaps in terms of language and content, thus tailoring the general course material to a specific classroom situation. Some of

The teacher as course book gap-filler

---

[12] Actually Andreas Siegfried Sachs, born 1930 in Berlin, whose family fled to Britain for obvious reasons in 1938. His latest role is as Ramsey Clegg in Coronation Street.

these gaps, however, are so large that it seems beyond the teacher's remit to bridge them. They are not merely information gaps in the course books; they constitute whole areas of life which are crucial to meaningful language acquisition but totally ignored in traditional teaching materials. Since these taboo subjects are not even hinted at, most teachers see no need to fill the gaps; indeed in some cases there are no gaps to fill, since the entire topic is missing. There are a number of these topics, but one of the most critical and most glaring deficiencies in regular course books is, as you have guessed, sex.

Let me make quite clear at this point that I am not referring to the language of profanities and the practice of swearing. That is a different topic entirely, and would require a chapter to itself. I am talking about sex. Leaving stage comedy aside, people do this quite a lot. They talk about sex. Newspapers are full of reports about who is doing what to whom. Soap operas without shagging would be, if you will forgive the pun, the biggest turn-off for both audience and production company. Native English speakers have a fine-tuned sense of double entendre and in a relaxed social situation often detect sexual innuendo in quite innocently uttered remarks, often to the total bewilderment of any non-native speakers present. After all, sex is not only the basis of human life; it is the bedrock of humour.

We need more humour in the classroom...

Consequently, we need more humour in the classroom. And we need more sex.

...and we need more sex.

I recall that very early on in my teaching career, I was approached after one particular lesson by two of the more attractive female students, both as it turned out divorcees and both with a common interest; they had joined the conversation course because they frequently went on holiday together and often found that English was the lingua franca of their holiday destinations. Their language course, they told me, was fine as far as it went, and the course book (which I was obliged to use) was okay, too, but they wanted something a little... well, a little 'different', something 'more'. I agreed to give them a couple of private lessons. (By the way, I will leave all the innuendo and double-entendre in this story to you, since there is no way to avoid them.) Clearly, they had realised that there were a few

Private lessons for private moments

things they wanted to learn but felt they couldn't ask in class, and a couple of private lessons, they quite rightly reasoned, would be an ideal way to fill these gaps. Accordingly, we had a couple of very pleasant sessions together (threesomes, if you like), the content of which involved quite a lot of flirting and dating, to say nothing of chat-up lines, put-downs and come-ons, everything in fact from 'have you got a light?' to the morning after. Well, maybe not quite everything, but enough for their purposes.

All this was very confidential, of course, and did not get fed back into the classroom during their course, but I subsequently incorporated some of the impromptu material into my regular teaching portfolio, bringing just a little more sex into the classroom on a regular basis. The biggest hurdle in doing this is, of course, the perceived danger of embarrassment, but as we have observed, sex and humour are so closely intertwined that the problem almost solves itself if you take a light-hearted approach.

Humour alleviates the embarrassment.

One of the most amazing things about the English language (and I would hazard to venture, British English in particular) is the vast number of euphemistic and jokey expressions we have for sexual activities, ranging from 'having it off' and 'getting your leg over' to many, much more graphic coinages, so clearly learners should be made aware of this language at some stage, but they also need to learn the clinical language, too, e.g. the relevant parts of the body. This is not only because they might need to discuss such matters in English, but because a fairly extensive passive vocabulary in this area can be crucial to understanding. Depending on the students L1, some of the terms may be obvious, but many will not. As a native or accomplished speaker of English, you, the teacher, will know what these items of language are, but that does not mean that it is easy to teach them. Have no fear; help is at hand.

The language of sex ranges from biology to euphemism.

Consider the following:

A: Now let's talk about testicles…

B: Balls to you.

A: What?

51

B: Testicles are sometimes called balls.

A: Oh, OK. Now, you might have heard that testicles...

B: Plums.

A: What?

B: Testicles are sometimes called plums...

Drawing EFL resource materials from TV sex education programmes

Where, you may ask, did this vocabulary explanation come from? Is this a somewhat clumsy English teacher trying to explain intimate details to an EFL class or is it a humorous exchange from a sitcom? Is it some form of 'adult material'? Far from it; this extract is taken from Channel 4's educational programme KNTV SEX, a ten-part series in which two animated 10-year olds, Kierky (Kierkegaard) and Nietzsche, run their own TV station from an abandoned government warehouse in Slabovia, the last communist state in Europe ('When the iron curtain fell, Slabovia was under it'). Their sexual discoveries combine zany humour with 3D imaging, archive footage, heavy metal guitar-bashing and subliminal satire in a 1984-type world inhabited by Svetlanas, Sex Spies and the sinister Burgess McPhilbin.

Slabovian Sex Guide

The series is ostensibly aimed at 14-19 year olds, but some of its target audience is actually younger, since it covers a fairly broad range from KS2/second level to KS4 and beyond)[13] and deals with a wide range of topics, including

- The male body
- The female body
- The act of sex
- The rules of attraction
- Puberty
- Pregnancy, childbirth and parenthood
- Contraception and sexually transmitted infections
- Sexuality
- Fantasy, arousal and desire
- Relationships

Content of Channel 4's KNTV SEX programme

If you want to know more, you might like to check out the programme notes on the Channel 4 website, but Slabovia's own site is much more fun. This is where the Ministry of Sex has published its very own *Slabovian Sex Guide* (along with downloadable videos and Kierky and Nietzsche's Relationship Song).

Now, I am not saying that *KNTV SEX* will serve all your classroom needs in this area, but considering that this is only one of many readily-available sex education programmes and since many are accompanied by written material, there is plenty more where this came from. In fact, PSHE (Personal, Social and Health Education) is now an accepted element of the state school curriculum in Great Britain and covers a range of subjects such as drugs and sex, knowledge of which is considered to be fundamental to a young person's development.

---

[13] Key Stages are used in the UK to refer to the educational knowledge appropriate to learners of specific school years/age groups, e.g. KS3 = years 7-9/ages11-14, KS4 = years 10-11/ages 14-16.

Ministry of sex website

It therefore follows that the language (e.g. idioms, clinical vocabulary and euphemisms) of these topics are equally fundamental to language awareness amongst adult learners.

More adult material can be found on late-night comedy shows...

Further key sources of lesson material include late-night comedy shows such as *Two Pints of Lager and a Packet of Crisps, Coming of Age* and *Family Guy*. A carefully selected five-minute clip and/or a downloaded synopsis of any of these can easily provide you with enough material for a whole lesson. Of course, you will have to tailor it to suit your particular class and ... er.... fill in the gaps.

... and even the news.

Finally, it is a strange quirk of the show-business world that the BBC's biggest sex-related scandal as I write occurred when presenters Jonathan Ross and Russell Brand found themselves in the crossfire for making lewd and sexually explicit phone calls to the answering machine of a respected actor who was due to be interviewed on Russell Brand's radio show. Indeed, their manner was considered so offensive that the affair led to a three-month suspension for Ross and the resignation not only of Brand but also of Radio 2 Controller Lesley Douglas for allowing the show to go out unedited. The actor's name? Andrew Sachs. Yes, the same. Funny old world, isn't it?

References

http://www.bbc.co.uk/comedy/twopints/

http://www.channel4learning.com/support/programmenotes/micro/kntvsex/index.html

http://www.comedy.co.uk/guide/tv/coming_of_age

http://www.direct.gov.uk/en/Parents/Schoolslearninganddevelopment/ExamsTestsAndTheCurriculum/DG_4016665

http://www.fox.com/familyguy/

http://www.slabovia.tv

http://www.teachernet.gov.uk/pshe/

On your bike!

The secret to being a good English teacher

The following thousand words or so will probably make me very unpopular with teacher trainers, teachers' associations and, I dare say, publishers. So I will summarise this chapter before they have had a chance to stop me: chuck away this book and go and do something else instead.

The Orwellian teacher

What makes a good teacher?

Still here? OK, then maybe you need a little more convincing. Much of the debate in the field of ELT professional development, both in print and at workshops and conferences, focuses on whether a good EFL/ESL teacher should be an instructor, mentor, organiser, prompter, facilitator, leader, arbitrator, role model, participant, consultant, resource centre or whatever. Sadly, a large part of this discussion misses the point, because in addition to the role of gap-filler discussed in the previous chapter, there is another role that never seems to be on any of these lists. Ironically, if you take a straw poll of practising teachers (try it at your next ELTA meeting) and ask which is better, teacher-centred or learner-centred, they will all cry 'learner-centred good, teacher-centred bad' and then prove it by telling you what they do in class to achieve this – what they, the teachers, do. Duh!

Various roles played by the English teacher

The China syndrome

But so far I have failed to digress, so indulge me now. Some years ago, when I had a much heavier teaching load than at present (and certainly no time to write about it), I decided to put myself in the position of my learners. I wanted to experience what it was like for them when they went to the UK or the USA for the first time and were confronted by real-life language challenges. I could hardly do this in Europe because although I may not be proficient, I can read or speak enough European languages to get by in most places and will probably be spoken to in English in any case. So I went to China. This was not the China of the Olympic Games and a strong, defiant currency; this was the China of blue tunics and Foreign Exchange Certificates – a pre-McDonald's and pre-Nestlé world in which a piece of candied fruit on a stick counted as a luxury in downtown Beijing, a world in which no-one outside a few tourist hotels spoke English.

Striving to be a learner...

The experiment was a success inasmuch as I was able to immerse myself in an alien environment in which I could neither read the signs outside shops and offices nor understand anything that I heard around me. But as I engrossed myself in the language, I soon realised that the whole venture was in fact a miserable failure – not because I couldn't learn Chinese, but because I could. I didn't find it particularly difficult to pick up sounds, learn vocabulary, recognize patterns and so on, and I quickly acquired some basic survival skills, setting myself tasks such as asking for directions, buying tickets, haggling with market traders and taxi drivers and so on. The problem was that even though the language and environment were unfamiliar, I was, unlike my students, still well within my comfort zone. After all, languages, as they say, is what I do.

... and failing.

Hitting the water

Back in Europe, I opted for a different approach and took up sailing, something about which I knew absolutely nothing. Of course, this also meant learning a new set of terminology and expressions, but more importantly, it involved acquiring totally new skills – not just pulling ropes and handling the wind, but

Changing tack...

57

... and succeeding. planning passages and navigating waters as vastly different as the Lake of Constance, the Mediterranean and the Solent. From the German boatmaster's licenses for sail and power to the RYA Coastal Skipper course, I did the lot, but in the odd days and weeks I could invest here and there in between my own teaching, I was never, ever, going to be anything more than a struggling tyro, way out of my depth with the guys who spend half of their lives on the water. But at least, I was learning.

Learning the ropes in the Med

A biker's tale

However, despite my unquestionable role as learner and novice, I found myself subconsciously observing and assessing the instructors, their methodologies and their general attitudes.

In some cases, their performance as instructors was of a somewhat lower order than their competence as sailors. Indeed, this should not come as a surprise to language teachers who, I hope, are aware that mere proficiency in a language (e.g. native speaker ability) has little or no bearing on the ability to teach it. At one particular sailing school,[14] however, I encountered only patient, committed and highly competent instructors.

'Do you,' I asked one of them as we tacked up the Hamble one day, 'have any special training apart from the usual instructor's qualifications?'

'Not really,' he replied, 'but last year I had to learn to ride a motorbike.' The school's Principal,[15] it seems, insisted that his teachers periodically immerse themselves in some new activity or learn some new skill – simply to make sure that they never forgot what it was like to be a learner. 'Well,' I mused, spinning the helm vigorously and dodging the boom, 'sailing is my motorbike.'

Learn to be a learner again!

Windy day in the Solent

---

[14] Southern Sailing, Southampton
[15] John Goode, a name not unknown in the UK sailing fraternity

Take to the sky

It isn't knowledge, but attitude that makes a good teacher.

It was reassuring to discover, albeit by a rather circuitous route, that I was not alone in my madness. It isn't knowledge that makes a good teacher; it's attitude – and the key to this is to stop trying to be a teacher and start understanding your learners. Good teachers are not instructors, facilitators, mentors, or any of that. Good teachers are good learners. So if you want to be a better English teacher, forget ELT books and conferences, and take up sailing, flying or skydiving instead.

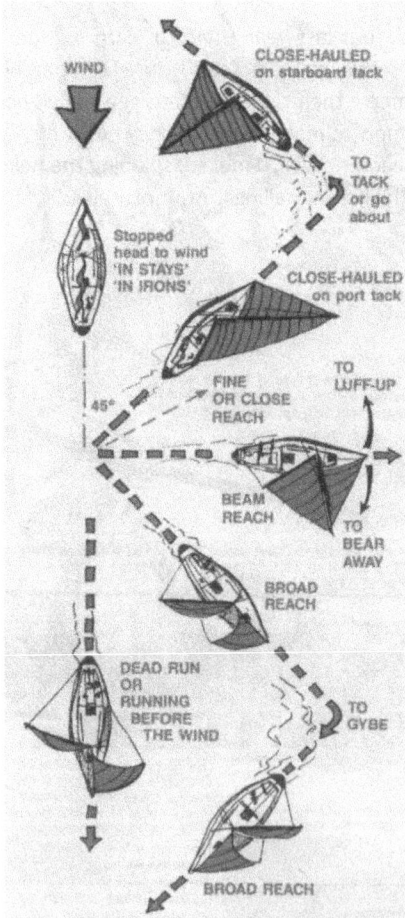

Ongoing learning: new skills and new terminology

© Royal Yachting Association

Why most teachers are sluts

Do native speakers really make better EFL teachers?

Have you ever found yourself just one step ahead of your students? What do you do, for example, when faced with a brand new course book? Read the whole thing through before you start? Of course not. You flick through the pages, glance at the contents and maybe check out the reference section to get an overall feel for the book, then you either plunge right in or you prepare the first lesson. Life is too short and time is too precious to do anything else. One step ahead plus the ability to deal intelligently with questions and issues arising – in most cases, that's all that's needed. In order to be effective in the ELT classroom, you need to be able to teach, and you need to be able to draw on a pool of resources, both methodological and linguistic. You don't need to know everything – and you don't need to be a native speaker.

Busy teachers often have little time for lesson preparation.

It is time to revise some notions about the relative merits of native and non-native English speaker teachers (NESTs and non-NESTs).

NESTs and non-NESTs differ with regard to their language proficiency and teaching behaviour and can be equally good teachers on their own terms (Medgyes: 25). Ideally, NESTs and non-NESTS should work together to complement their skills (Claypole 2005: 7) and each should benefit from the particular advantages and insights of the other, but in practice, these two groups of teachers tend to live and work in quite different environments. Consequently, there is much less professional exchange than there might be. Ironically, it is the NESTs who are disadvantaged by this, since non-native teachers of English are almost by definition in a position to study the latest educational theories printed in English as well as in their own language, whilst many NESTs, particularly those residing in English-speaking countries, are unlikely to ever benefit from research published in, let's say, Chinese or Russian.

Native-speaker teachers and non-native speaker teachers should ideally work together.

Native-user teachers – handle with care

Native-language ability does not necessarily mean more effective teaching.

My main contention here is that there is no automatic correlation between native language ability and effective teaching. Clearly, some English teachers know more English than others, but then some geography teachers know more geography than others without necessarily being better teachers. In other words, there is no objective reason to suppose that a native speaker is per se a better teacher than a non-native; on the contrary, in many teaching situations, the prerequisites for effective teaching are more likely to reside with the non-native. Here we once again return to the central issue of the teacher's role, since any assessment of the effectiveness of a teacher depends on how we view that teacher's role in a specific situation. At various times, a teacher of any given subject may be expected to act as a representative of society, judge, resource, helper, referee, detective, object of identification, limiter of anxiety, ego-supporter, group leader or parent surrogate (Hoyle: 59-60) whilst the role of the EFL/ESL teacher has also been likened to that of a controller, assessor, organiser, prompter, participant, and investigator (Harmer: 58ff). Equally, a language teacher may be a role model (e.g. for pronunciation), a facilitator (encouraging dialogue and instigating learning situations) or even a co-learner:

I recall once overhearing an erstwhile colleague of mine taking her first Business English class; she opened the book, looked at an exercise on financial vocabulary and said to the students, 'I don't know this stuff either. Let's learn it together, shall we?'

But despite all these various roles, a lot of teaching, even language teaching, involves the imparting and disseminating of knowledge. And in many cases, non-NESTs are better at communicating information about the language. For one thing, non-NESTs are generally better at grammar, since they have in most cases made a formal study of it. Where NESTs generally excel in communicative skills, non-NESTS are better at conveying formal knowledge and content. Whereas a communicative syllabus profits from the advantages of the NEST, non-NESTS are more readily able to deal with the emerging demand for content and language integrated learning (CLIL). Indeed, non-NESTs bring many excellent qualities to the classroom. Generally speaking, they can

Non-NESTs are better at teaching formal knowledge and content...

- provide a good learner model for imitation;
- teach language learning strategies more effectively;
- supply learners with more information about the English language;
- anticipate and prevent language difficulties better;
- be more empathetic to the needs and problems of learners;
- make use of the learners' mother tongue. (Medgyes: 48)

I have illustrated in the previous chapter that good teachers need to be good learners, and one characteristic that all non-NESTs have in common is the ability to learn a language other than their own. This fact alone does not make them good learners, but it certainly puts them in a position to provide a learner model for imitation in a way that a NEST, having not consciously learned the target language as an adult, frequently can not. Indeed, it has been argued that only non-NESTs can set proper learning models, since they learned English after they acquired their native language. Thus, learning, not acquisition, should be at the centre of a language teacher's strategy (Bao: 8).

... because they have learned it themselves.

Before taking my arguments further, I would like to address the matter of terminology. In this context, most commentators use the terms NEST and non-NEST (or NNEST). However, I find that this places rather too much emphasis on the skill of speaking. Indeed, it is a widespread misconception that if you can speak a language as a native, you can also write it. And whilst it may suit advocates of the communicative approach to equate language competence with the ability to speak, writing skills are far more closely related to formal education than to oral competence, and many non-natives are better at writing than the average native speaker. For want of a better term, I shall therefore refer not to native speakers but to native users of a language and have therefore coined the term 'native user teacher' (NUT) to refer to a person who is teaching his or her own native language, whether it is English or any other language. Logically, therefore, anyone who is teaching a language other than their own mother tongue should be referred to as a 'second language user teacher' (SLUT).

Writing skills are related to formal education — not to speaking skills.

In the *ETM* article on which this chapter is based, I played out this joke to the full, using lower-case letters for these acronyms when comparing and contrasting the select band of 'nuts' to the 'sluts' who make up the majority of language teachers world wide (hence the title of this chapter). However, since the pejorative connotations of the word 'slut' make it unlikely to gain wider currency, I shall shorten the acronym here to SUT.

Much more importantly, there is a key distinction to be made between non-NESTs and SUTs. It will later become clear that the L1 of the SUT need not be the same as that of the student. Many of the advantages enjoyed by the second language user of the students' L2, such as bilingualism, greater formal knowledge, heightened empathy, are equally valid for second language users of English with a different L1 to that of the students. What is more, in order to be a proficient second language user, it is not necessary to be a native user of the student's language. Outside NES countries, many teachers in the private sector are, in fact, native users of English who are highly proficient in the L1 of their students. In other words, NUTs and SUTs are not mutually exclusive. Having said that, however, experience indicates that the majority of NUTs who are also SUTs tend to model their teaching behaviour on that of the typical NUT rather than avail

The L1 of a second language user teacher need not be the same as that of the students.

themselves of the potential advantages of being, as it were, a part-time SUT. Typically, for example, they make little use of their second language (the students' L1) in class, and base their methodology on that of the monolingual NUT.

Research has shown that while NUTs are more innovative and flexible in their teaching, SUTs are more insightful, empathetic and sensitive to the students' real needs (cf. Medgyes: 61). This should not be surprising, since in many cases they have learned a language in a formalised way that is familiar to the students, but not to the NUTs. Whilst NUTs tend to focus on fluency, meaning, oral skills and colloquial register, SUTs pay more attention to accuracy, form, grammar, writing and formal registers.

NUTs are more innovative and flexible, but SUTs show greater insight and more empathy.

And here, perhaps, lies the nub; what makes a better teacher in any given context depends on a number of factors, ranging from the location (whether in an ESL or an EFL country), the learning objective (travel, exams, business, research) and the student profile (age, social status, educational background).

Let me therefore put my forgoing remarks in the context of teaching English in Germany. Leaving political considerations aside, German-born teachers are in many ways better equipped than NUTs to deal with the German exam syllabus and school system. Amongst ex-pats, tales abound of the children of native speakers being corrected by 'ignorant' or 'incompetent' non-native user teachers, but such slip-ups are the exception rather than the rule and although they loom large in the minds of the (already linguistically competent) children and their parents, have little or no effect on the overall success of a course of instruction, and minor teacher errors pale into absolute insignificance when we look at the big picture in which English is being taught as one school subject amongst many to a wide range of different types of learner. Apart from the fact that within the school system, the non-native user is teaching English within the constraints of a formalised environment, there are in any case not enough native user teachers to go around. And whether language purists like it or not, a school teacher has a job to do and a large part of that job is to get the kids through their exams, not to equip them with a quasi-native awareness of the target language.

Local teachers understand the system and the culture.

In the communicative model, we are tolerant of student mistakes, so why should we pounce on teacher errors? As part of an overall package in which the student is exposed to native speakers through audio-visual materials in the classroom and mass media outside it, the teacher's role as a model of perfection is largely supplanted by the role of facilitator. In a multimedia society, a teacher can be expected to teach without providing the only model. Gone are the days when all students would simply mimic the RP of their teachers. Nowadays they are more likely to imitate Brad Pitt or Amy Winehouse (or whichever showbiz icons are currently in favour). Incidentally, it is often overlooked that unless they are pro-active, NUTs who live abroad can themselves very quickly become rusty in their language use and find their native language competence impaired. It is not unusual for expats to unconsciously adopt the attitudes of their chosen community and to lose touch with their origins. As an example of this, I was recently in conversation with an experienced EFL teacher who, although she is a native speaker of English, was totally unaware of the current use of 'well' as an intensifier in such expressions as 'well good' or 'well fit'. Accordingly, she had been correcting her teenage students for using these forms, telling them that 'well' could not be used in this way.

Even native speaker teachers must keep their language skills up to date.

Now let us move on to the adult ELT sector in Germany. Here the constraints and goals are quite different to those of state schools. In this area, it is not so much exams but business, technology and specific content that dominate the students' needs. In the tertiary sector, the Bologna process and the transition from diploma courses to bachelor's and master's degrees, together with an increased emphasis on content and language integrated learning (CLIL) have boosted the number of German speaking subject teachers who are required to lecture or give instruction through the medium of English, a task that in many cases requires a high degree of specialisation in which language competence is a relatively minor consideration. A non-specialist NUT would have very few advantages over an experienced and specialised SUT. After all, if you are studying mechatronics, agriculture or medical engineering, you need in-depth understanding of your subject and its terminology, not perfect pronunciation and a fine sense of colloquial nuance.

For CLIL, knowledge of the subject is more important than native speaker ability.

In the private sector, too, SUTs are on the increase and in what is probably the most significant shift in perception in recent years, now enjoy an acceptance amongst students, human resources managers and course organisers that would have been unthinkable only a few years ago. At LinguaServe, for example, we now employ more SUTs than NUTs. This is not a policy shift, but simply reflects changing needs and demographic developments. In fact, we not only employ native German speakers to teach English, but also engage Polish, Spanish and Czech citizens to teach not just English, but also German, both in our school and in company, and with great success. It should also be said that we not only look very carefully at the qualifications and teaching skills of our SUTs, but also attach a great deal of weight to the German language skills of our NUTs. There are indeed a great many NUTs who also qualify as SUTs by virtue of being regular and accomplished users of the students' L1 besides being native users of English, whilst in addition to the ones mentioned above, our teachers of German also include Russian, Rumanian and Serbian citizens.

In Europe, people are on the move.

In fact, this brief overview barely scrapes the surface of what is an intricate and extremely varied set of teaching parameters and learning goals. As a consequence of European enlargement, our student base in Germany is no longer homogeneous, but also includes second generation immigrants who are already bilingual or quasi-native in at least one language other than German, with English being their third, or in some cases, fourth language. In this increasingly complex climate of demographic change, the additional language skills of the native teacher are of much less importance than proven pedagogical skills and professionalism.

Professionalism and good teaching skills are more important than native speaker competence.

Welcome to the new Europe and the age of the SUTs.

References
Bao, T. (2008) *Suiting the Medicine to the Illness: TEFL in a Foreign Language Learning Context*, TEFL China
Claypole, M. (2005) 'Working Together – Native and Non-native EFL Teachers' in *EFL World*, April Issue
Harmer, J. (2001) *The Practice of English Language Teaching*, Longman
Hoyle, E. (1969) *The Role of the Teacher*, Routledge
Medgyes, P. (1999) *The non-native teacher*, Max Hueber Verlag

Myth or magic?

Technology and parapsychology in ELT

Virtual learning environments, Moodles, 3D digital worlds, e-tutoring systems, interactive whiteboards, Web 2.0, m-lessons: on the face of it, there seems to be no end to the host of new technologies currently being introduced for language learning and teaching. Indeed, I am a keen user of such innovations myself and have frequently reported on them in various publications.

New delivery platforms do not constitute a new pedagogy...

On closer inspection, however, these technologies are mostly nothing more than alternative forms of delivery. An interactive whiteboard, for example, is an innovative way to present material in class and would appear to offer several advantages over a purely physical board, but for language teaching, it is far from indispensable, since it is, in effect, nothing more than a giant touch screen and as such is entirely dependent for its success on other factors such as the software, the lesson content, preparation and planning and – well, just about everything in fact.

... and may run contrary to sound pedagogical reasoning.

The same applies to most other technologies. They do not constitute a pedagogy in any real sense at all, and in many cases their implementation runs contrary to sound pedagogical practice, since they either offer the user a bewildering array of unnecessary options or they lack the focus and structure which is conducive to learning and language acquisition. At worst, they merely become new versions of what is in effect an electronic delivery platform for paper-based techniques such as gap-fills, quizzes and crosswords. In many cases, hi-tech solutions are used to overcome geographical hurdles or the inability to attend face-to-face lessons; but simply meeting up in Second Life, giving feedback via Camtasia or holding a Skype conference does not in itself constitute a teaching strategy. However, it was not always so. Let me take you back to a time when language learning technologies were more primitive, more cumbersome and used to much greater effect.

There was a time, not so long ago, when it was quite common to see display adverts in the press showing a reclining figure wearing a benevolent smile, the very epitome of relaxation, generally sporting a discreet facemask and earphones. The caption under the picture would reveal, in the local language, 'I'm not sleeping. I'm learning English.' On offer was a language learning program marketed as the 'SITA Learning System'. The system combined a variety of relaxation techniques with audio recordings: a new way to learn – fast, efficiently and effortlessly. It was based on a technique known as 'Superlearning'.

Relaxation and learning

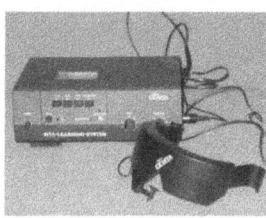

The SITA Learning System

My interest in Superlearning dates back to 1979 when Sheila Ostrander and Lynn Schroeder consolidated their studies on the work of Bulgarian researcher Georgi Lozanov. Lozanov is the acknowledged founder of suggestology a.k.a. suggestopaedia, accelerated learning or Superlearning, a form of relaxation-cum-learning which has gone through several phases of development since its initial introduction behind the iron curtain in the mid sixties. It should be said at the outset that suggestopaedia was not developed exclusively for language learning but as a means of rapidly assimilating snippets of knowledge quickly – and foreign-language vocabulary and phrases was one area to which this system seemed admirably suitable, especially in Eastern bloc countries where native speaker language teachers were relatively scarce. Consequently, the technique flourished in Lozanov's native Bulgaria and in the then Soviet Union. When the West began to show interest, however, there was a great deal of hush about the 'true recipe' for success. Many, mainly Western, visitors to Bulgaria had witnessed impressive demonstrations, but failed to implement the techniques successfully on their return to their own countries. Eventually, the reason for this emerged: Those who had simply wanted to poach a good idea for free had been shown an incomplete version, with key elements of the

Suggestopaedia was developed as a way of assimilating snippets of information quickly.

process not explained; others, such as the government of East Germany, had paid for the privilege of receiving a fuller demonstration and were duly let into the trade secrets. Accordingly, they too reported an increase in learning in terms of vocabulary and language acquisition. My own experiments at the time involved designing practice sessions to enhance basic vocabulary in Farsi but were too small in scale for any meaningful conclusions to be drawn.

Superlearning schools founded

In Eastern Europe, however, statistics were published which indicated a rapid acceleration in learning and the West, too, systems became more sophisticated and soon Superlearning schools were springing up everywhere. The key to the success, it was discovered, was not merely to induce a state of relaxation prior to gently imbuing the learner with sound recordings of the words and phrases to be learnt, but scientific studies had shown that a state of enhanced receptiveness was created by the use of specific rhythms. It was not enough for the relaxation music to be simply soothing; it must have a beat slightly slower than the human heart in order to induce the required physiological and mental state. In musical terms, this technique therefore favoured a largo (40 to 60 beats per minute) typical of much of Baroque music, thus tapping into a hidden area of expertise of the likes of J. Bach, Handel and Vivaldi. Similarly, the pace at which the information was fed to the learner was critical – sixty beats with an eight to ten second activity cycle – and the use of alternating speakers were essential to success. The scientific basis of Lozanov's technique was therefore much more involved than had been appreciated, and only a carefully developed course of relaxation and learning would achieve the sought-after increase in learning. Numerous studies attested to the success of the system in the East, and a further wave of commercial ventures followed, implementing the full system in the West. Of course, it still didn't work. As a result, some people wasted a little time, others lost money and maybe a few reputations were tarnished, but as a major force, the technique, like Lozanov himself, faded into near obscurity.

The secret was to use the right beat...

... and to carefully control the flow of information...

... but it still didn't work.

Why? For the simple reason that it was all bunkum from the start. Hocus pocus, if you like; snake oil of the first order.

Despite the repeated repetition of Lozanov's self-proclaimed successes and constant reference to such evidence as the Superlearning/Ebbinghaus memory retention curve comparison, none of Lozanov's results have ever been duplicated or reliably authenticated by independent research or empirical study.

The graph shown below has often been used to illustrate the effectiveness of Superlearning by plotting the rate at which

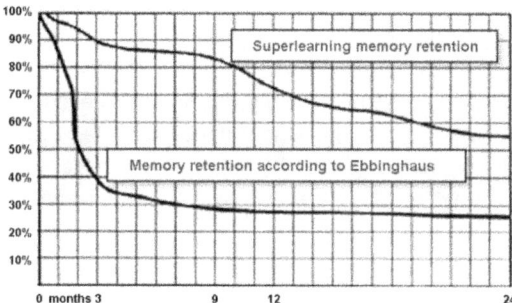

Impressive evidence of success...

Apocryphal memory retention results claimed for Superlearning (Source: PLS LernStudio, Munich, after Lozanov)

learners forget content against a non-suggestopaedic benchmark (Ebbinghaus), but information about what precisely was measured by Lozanov and under what conditions is hard to come by. What is known, however, is that Ebbinghaus's work (first published in 1885) did not involve the study of foreign languages at all, but tested how well the subject (himself) was able to memorise nonsense syllables. For this reason alone, the comparison is hardly a fair one. And it certainly does not compare Superlearning to other forms of language teaching.

... can be misleading.

Indeed, one suspects that the much-cited success statistics from Lozanov's Institute of Suggestology were a combination of wishful thinking, publication bias and cherry picking, a technique used by overenthusiastic researchers throughout the ages; you carry out a lot of studies, publish the ones that support your ideas and bin the rest. And if you keep your methods secret or incorporate so many variables that your results are not reproducible anyway, who's to know? As any true scientist appreciates, the only research results that you should believe are the ones that are reliably and independently reproducible.

... or are there lessons to be learned?

Of course, the system has not entirely gone away. Manufacturers of relaxation chairs frequently offer language learning packages as part of their marketing strategy, and there is a considerable demand for other relaxation devices, too, from alpha-wave and biofeedback systems to face masks, light machines, sound therapy and even olfactory stimulus devices. Indeed, Superlearning schools still exist (and I note that the 'I'm not sleeping' slogan has reappeared, too) and let me say categorically that it is not my purpose here to detract from their work or belittle their techniques. On the contrary, I believe there are lessons to be learned from the Superlearning experience – lessons that go beyond the mere process of debunking a myth. This is what makes the whole matter such a fascinating and complex issue. Hang on to your headsets, because there is a sense in which Superlearning in its post-Lozanov form can actually work.

Current advertisement claiming, 'I'm not sleeping! I'm learning English.' (Source: Alpha College AG, Berlin)

I said at the outset that most of what nowadays passes as learning technology is nothing more than a delivery platform. Superlearning is not like that. It is a pedagogical theory that at its best harnesses the technology of the day in order to achieve learning goals. In Lozanov's day, this technology consisted mainly of comfy chairs and tape recorders. Nowadays, thanks to presentation software, data projectors, plasma screens, DVD, Blu-ray and the internet, we have many more toys to play with.

A means to an end

The fact that an idea or technique may lack a truly scientific basis and may indeed be based on a total fiction does not mean that it can't be harnessed as an aid to language learning. A lot of the grammar currently being taught is apocryphal nonsense, but it is useful for teaching because it is one way of condensing the mechanics of a language into digestible chunks. And it doesn't actually do students any harm to believe that there is such a thing as a perfect tense in English or a some/any rule. By the time they realize that it is all smoke and mirrors, they will have learnt so much of the language anyway that it no longer matters.

Superlearning draws on this phenomenon. As a technique, it is no better than any other, but in many cases, it is no worse either. Let's take some basic items of vocabulary, for example: chair, table, book, fridge, freezer, blue, green, apple, orange, big, little, file, directory, cut, paste, helicopter, submarine, amphibious landing craft, whatever. If you want to learn these words in a foreign language, it does not matter whether you learn them from a teacher flapping his or her arms about in a monolingual class, from a bilingual course book or from an audio recording. They are discrete items of knowledge. Of course, there are aspects of usage that must also be learnt, false correlations to be avoided and so on, but this applies however the initial lexical base is acquired. Suggestopaedia is a useful method of learning vocabulary. It may or may not be the best method, but in any particular case, the choice of method depends on the alternatives available. In Soviet-era Eastern bloc countries, the shortage of native English speakers, let alone qualified language teachers, from whom to learn items of vocabulary directly, made the technology of language labs and Superlearning classes a logical choice. The same applies in many developing countries today. The explosion of English as a lingua franca leaves many countries struggling to find enough teachers for their needs. A partially automated method can easily help to fill this gap.

Suggestopaedia is a useful way of learning vocabulary.

Ultimately, there is no point in focussing on contrastive issues, i.e. on whether Superlearning per se is better or worse than any other method, since such an exclusive attitude would imply that as teacher or learner you employ one method of teaching or learning to the exclusion of all others. Surely, it is much more reasonable to ask whether any given technique, Superlearning included, can be used in conjunction with other methods as part of a comprehensive learning program. And here, too, the answer is: yes, it can.

Superlearning is just one tool amongst many.

Superlearning is Web 2.0 compatible...

Above all, Superlearning is Web 2.0 compatible. In a recent blended learning course developed by LinguaServe to teach English for industrial relations, we incorporated our own version of a more pro-active type of Superlearning (we call them EasyLearn™ sessions) into the software introduction to each learning unit. In other words, our Trade Union Interactive course combines Superlearning and Web 2.0. Although it is only one of many techniques employed in this package, the Superlearning component has proven to be an unmitigated success – not according to the results of any statistical analysis – but according to a very different criteria altogether – student feedback. Our students love it; it lets them start each session with a feelgood factor, and happy students are better learners. In addition, happy distance learning students spend more time using the program than they would do otherwise and therefore learn more. In other words, Superlearning is not really a science and certainly not a panacea but used wisely, it works.

... and students love it!

References

Ebbinghaus, H. (1913) *Memory. A Contribution to Experimental Psychology*. Teachers College, Columbia University, New York

Lozanov, G., Balevsky, P. and Trashliev, R. (1969) *Basic Trends and Methods of our Experimental Suggestological Investigations*. Institute of Suggestology, Bulgaria

Lozanov, G. and Balevsky, P. (1975) 'The Effect of the Suggestopedic System of Instruction on the Physical Development, State of Health and Working Capacity of First and Second Grade Pupils' in *Suggestology and Suggestopedia, Vol. 1. No. 3*

Ostrander, S., Ostrander, N. and Schroeder, L. (1979) *Superlearning*. Delacorte Press, New York

Wozniak, R. H. (1999) 'Introduction to Memory; Hermann Ebbinghaus (1885/1913)' in *Classics in Psychology, 1855-1914: Historical Essays*, Bristol

http://superlearning.com
http://arbeitsblaetter.stangl-taller.at/LERNEN/Superlearning.gif
http://www.sprachen-mit-erfolgsgarantie.de
http://www.pls-lernstudio.com/index.htm
http://linguaserve.biz/tui

Not such a poor relation
The role of translation in language teaching

The practice of translation for teaching purposes is inextricably bound up with the use of L1 in the classroom. Over the past few decades it has become axiomatic that since language is a form of communication, language teaching requires a communicative approach. Interaction between students is encouraged and the main emphasis is on fluency and active language production. Discourse management and non-verbal communication are key factors in measuring the learning curve as students progress from fairly simple, everyday tasks to more complex ones requiring an ever-deepening cultural awareness. Classroom activities and teaching strategies are designed to focus on the interactive functions of the language being learned, whilst student motivation derives from the successful completion of real-life tasks.

The communicative approach has established itself in the language classroom...

In this dynamic, functional, task-based environment, there is no place for the students' own language; indeed the use of anything other than English in the classroom is often frowned upon by language schools, human resources officers, teachers and even the students themselves.

... leaving no place for the students' own language.

The communicative mind set

When asked why the use of Japanese is strictly forbidden in his schools and why only native English speakers are used, the educational director of a chain of private language schools in Japan replied:

The use of L1 in the classroom is often forbidden.

> 'For 6 days and 23 hours of the week, our students live in a Japanese world. For only one hour a week, they should have an English intensive lesson. It may be their only opportunity to hear a native English speaker, so why should that native English speaker use Japanese when they could be hearing perfect English?' (Klevberg 2000)

CONTROVERSIES IN ELT

In the communicative paradigm the teacher does not have to speak the students' L1.

The teacher is not expected to use the students' first language in class; indeed there is no requirement for the teacher to be able to speak it at all. The goal is for the learners to 'think in English' and any form of translation in the classroom is actively discouraged. There are a number of reasons for this attitude, most of them historical, none of them good.

I would argue that in cases like this the communicative approach has got out of control. Moreover, the communicative credo has caused the baby to be thrown out with the bathwater – the baby in this case being the use of translation as an aid to teaching.

Translation has been turned out of the classroom...

Translation in the ELT classroom

In my view, we cannot ban translation from the ELT classroom for the simple reason that all learners are to some degree translators. Adult students of English learn largely by translating what they read and hear into their own language, regardless of what the teacher does. Apart from absolute beginners, all students are familiar with at least two languages and quickly become accustomed to negotiating meaning between them.

... but language learners are translators.

The extent to which the teacher can benefit from this depends largely on the linguistic homogeneity of the student base and the teacher's own knowledge of the students' language. If classes are taking place in an English-speaking country, the teacher will probably be a native speaker of English, whereas the students may come from a variety of language backgrounds. In this case, the use of translation in the classroom will be limited since English is probably the only language that teachers and students have in common. Outside such countries, however, the situation is very different. In many parts of the world, local teachers are not native speakers of English but share a common L1 with the students (cf. pages 61ff). Alternatively, the teacher may be a native speaker of English with a greater or lesser command of the language of the host country.

Location, location, location

Monolingual methodologies developed for teaching English in the English-speaking world are inadequate and inappropriate in non-English speaking countries. Here, the most suitable methodological package will depend on a number of local factors such as the structural closeness of English to L1, the potential for exposure to English outside the classroom and of course the teacher's own language skills. Above all, **the constraints placed on teachers who do not speak the students' native language should not become a restriction on those who do.**

Traditional grammar/translation method

Translation is the oldest method of learning a second language and has been applied throughout the ages for deciphering foreign writing or communicating through an interpreter with speakers of other languages. Together with a study of formal grammar, translation is the traditional method for acquainting pupils with the Classics. Much of the negative reputation of the use of translation as a teaching aid results from a mistaken association with the grammar/translation method.

Translation is the traditional method of learning a second language.

The grammar/translation method is often seen as a way of developing the students' appreciation of literature, a technique which involves presenting learners with literary texts for translation and requiring them to memorize grammar rules and native-language equivalents of L2 vocabulary. (Snow 1992) And this indeed is how languages were taught until well into the nineteenth century. What I find horrifying is the underlying acceptance that this is the ONLY way to use translation in the classroom. The fact that is often overlooked is that **whereas you can not practice the grammar/translation method without using translation, you can use translation without practicing the grammar/translation method.**

The grammar/ translation method is not the only way to use translation.

The demise of translation in ELT

Translation has generally fallen into disuse in ELT as a result of two major influences – one theoretical, the other more grounded in situational expedience.

Current so-called communicative practices in ELT have developed over a period of time and have been subject to a number of influences, not least of which is Stephen D. Krashen's

Where did it all go wrong?

1981 paper on the principles of second language acquisition. Inasmuch as it is possible to set a particular date when things went horribly wrong, this is probably it.

Krashen's distinction between acquisition and learning

Krashen distinguishes between two ways that adults can develop competence in a language: acquisition and learning. Acquisition is a subconscious process similar to the way a child learns language without being aware of any grammatical rules. In other words, acquisition means 'picking-up a language'. Language learning, on the other hand, refers to the 'conscious knowledge of a second language, knowing the rules, being aware of them, and being able to talk about them.' (Krashen 1981)

Krashen points out that people throughout history have acquired, rather than learned, second languages while they were concentrating on the task in hand, e.g. gaining information, or interacting with people. What he doesn't say, is that they had no choice. They didn't have a teacher. What they did have was time. Today this situation is reversed. Especially in the rapidly growing fields of Business English, Technical English and Content Integrated Language Learning, adult learners simply do not have the time to wait until they have assimilated the language they need through a combination of trial and error, stimulus and reinforcement and self-correction.

Learning a second language is not the same as learning the first.

Methodologies based on Krashen's premises make the false assumption that learning a second language is akin to learning the first. It isn't. Adults learning a second language have quite different mental patterns and different learning curves to children and they already have a first language with which to organise their thoughts. It is unnatural to suppress this valuable skill and resource.

Commercial considerations played a key role.

A further reason for the demise of translation as a teaching tool and the rise of the direct method and subsequently the audio-lingual and communicative approaches is that market forces required a rapid expansion of the teacher base. Using the direct method or a communicative variant thereof, new teachers can be equipped with enough skills to get them started, irrespective of where they end up teaching. This has led to many inexperienced teachers being actively discouraged from using the students' L1 and consequently developing the idea that it is actually wrong to do so. *(Owen 2003)*

This combination of commercial interests and purist attitudes on the part of many native speaker teachers has been referred to rather cynically as 'linguistic imperialism' and its consequences as the 'monolingual fallacy'. (Canagarajah 1999)

Linguistic imperialism and the monolingual fallacy

By training teachers to become effective without using the students' own language, **monolingual methodologies totally overlook a valuable resource possessed by those teachers who DO speak the students' language.**

Translation is a real-life skill

Although the traditional grammar/translation methodology is in many ways highly inappropriate to today's tasks, the practice of translation is still a valuable resource in the modern classroom. Not to use it would be extremely wasteful. Furthermore, students do it all the time. Learners find it useful and there is no point in telling them to stop or to 'think in English'. In many cases, translation is one of the things that students actually need to do in the real world beyond the classroom.

Translation is a valuable resource.

I recently collected over 50 different types of translation, ranging from semantic, communicative and cognitive to situational, cultural and formulaic. And there is a wide range of skills and activities involved. To translate a source text, the translator must first establish the main purpose, understand fine detail, infer meaning from the context, and extract key information, then accurately decode the source language, resolve any ambiguities, reformulate the information as well as possibly substitute cultural equivalents, omit any superfluous information, expand for clarification, explain any incongruities and even adapt the content, check and correct the text and finally verify the suitability of the translation for the intended purpose. The translator may be required to show a general overall understanding, to balance accuracy against coherence and to demonstrate mastery of idiomatic usage.

There are many types of translation, involving a wide range of skills.

In short, translation is a complex process, but this does not mean that English teachers can not exploit it. On the contrary, this indicates just how great the scope for exploitation is.

What makes a good translation?

Whereas most people can identify a bad translation, opinions differ on what constitutes a good one. Should it reflect the wording of the original or the underlying ideas? Should it convey the style of the source culture or of the target language? Are additions or omissions permissible? And so on. In practice, all options are open because no translation has any meaning without a context and a purpose. For example, if the purpose is to test a student's knowledge of the source language, then a good translation would demonstrate this knowledge; adherence to the detail without omissions or embellishments would be expected. However, if the aim is to produce operating instructions for a machine, then a good translation would facilitate use of the machine, regardless of the degree of adherence to the source text.

Translation as a method of language teaching

Translation is a communicative activity and is lexical in nature.

Translating is essentially a communicative activity and it is largely lexical in nature and is compatible with other methodologies. Professional translators do not concern themselves mainly with single words, but tend to translate passages chunk by chunk. And it can provide a point of departure for task-based or discovery learning.

Valeria Petrocchi of the University for Foreigners at Perugia in Italy expands on the notion of 'pedagogic translation':

> 'Teaching English is closely tied to teaching translation methods. Translation is a useful tool to learn grammar, syntax, and lexis in both [source language] and [target language]. ... translating is a sort of re-writing. ... Since the text has its own identity, it must respect the rules which govern its language. When students translate, they unconsciously follow three steps: analysis, transfer, and restructuring.' (Petrocchi 2006)

In practice, the decision whether or not to include a translation component in a language course will depend largely on **who** the learners are, **why** they are learning the language, **where** the lessons are taking place, **what** should be taught and **how** it should be taught.

The **how** results from a clear understanding of the **who**, **why**, **where** and the **what**. It would be foolhardy to exclude any of the wealth of methodologies and activities available on purely ideological grounds. Successful teaching is not teaching that is fashionable, but teaching that works. If students benefit from an activity, it has a valuable role in the classroom. And of all the techniques at our disposal, the one that students of English instinctively try to master (even if repeatedly told that they shouldn't) is that of translation. It is also one of the most useful skills that can be acquired within the context of international and cross-cultural communication.

The challenge for the teacher

Of course, the fact that this technique is useful and flexible and that it helps the learner does not mean that it is easy on the teacher.

In addition to asking the questions outlined above, each teacher needs to practice a little soul-searching relating to the topic of translation:

Who am I? Am I a native speaker of English? Do I have mastery of the students' L1? Am I stronger in one language than the other? Do my students sometimes know more than I do?

What skills do I have? Do I write with ease and confidence in both languages? Do I constantly keep my knowledge and skills up to date? Am I a competent translator? Can I recognise a good translation when I see one? Can I instinctively identify a poor translation? Can I identify the key elements of a lengthy passage and rephrase them? Can I read between the lines in the students' L1? Do I understand the workings of style and register? Can I discern ambiguities and treat them effectively in translation? Am I practised in terminology research? Am I aware of my hidden talents? Am I aware of my limitations?

These questions are only a guideline for self-discovery and professional development. We all have limitations and we all have

The way translation is implemented in the classroom depends on the skills of the teacher.

hidden talents. The key is to be honest with oneself and find the right balance of techniques for classroom use and possibly to improve one's own language skills in the process.

The teacher may know too much of the students' L1...

An accomplished speaker of both languages may find it easy to translate texts which will present great difficulties for students. In this case, the key challenge is to set translation tasks which match the needs and skills of the students. This may entail accepting student answers which are passable and fulfil the task, even though the teacher is capable of something much more elegant or advanced. The language classroom is a place for learners to learn, not for teachers to parade their skills.

... or very little.

But how can teachers with little or no knowledge of the students' language use translation as an aid to teaching? Such teachers could, for example, use material that has already been translated into English from the students' language. By comparing the students' efforts with the translation they can ensure that the overall meaning is right whilst correcting or commenting on any lexical, structural, stylistic or other errors. In addition, peer-group teaching can also take place. Fellow students may not have all the answers, but a little team work and research can go a long way.

The use of back translation

Back translations provide a further example of translation activities that do not necessarily require the teacher to be a translator. Both input and output are in English and although the teacher may not be able to follow all the processes involved, this kind of exercise can generate very useful class discussions. Furthermore, in an open and honest teaching environment, the students do not expect the teacher to know everything but will usually appreciate any effort being made to help them improve their bilingual skills, regardless of whether the teacher speaks their language or not. In fact, if the teacher does not speak the students' L1, many students will appreciate the effort even more.

Translation exercises are ideal for the self-study phase of a blended learning course.

Translation in a virtual classroom

Translation work is an ideal component of the distance learning element of a blended learning course. During self-study phases, most students work with bilingual dictionaries in any case, so adding translation tasks is merely an extension of what they are already doing. One-to-one equivalences of key vocabulary and phrases are not only an excellent way of learning meaningful vocabulary, they are extremely easy to program, store, monitor and evaluate. Free translation exercises on the other hand are much harder to quantify and recycle than cloze tests or multiple matching tasks, but since the process of active translation can in itself be time consuming and involve a considerable degree of silent work, the production phase is in fact quite suited to offline distance learning, whilst the active discussion phase can take place either face-to-face or in a text-based online forum such as an asynchronous blog or an online community. Indeed, community sites offer added scope for peer-to-peer enhancement of translation skills within the scope of a teacher-moderated hybrid learning concept. In short, translation work is a Facebook and Moodle compatible task and can easily be extended to incorporate activities within multilingual 3D environments such as Second Life.

Translation is suitable for a range of learning platforms.

In a separate publication I have suggested thirty-one ways to use translation in the classroom (Claypole, 2010). I can not list them all here, but would offer two general suggestions for classroom activities:

1. When translating into English, tell your students that you are using translation as a teaching aid and that the goal is not to produce a perfect translation, but to learn from the activity.

Guidelines for using translation in class

2. When translating into the student's L1, focus on the notion of decoding as an aid to understanding the English.

A valuable resource for the future

The bottom line of all this is that some measure of classroom translation work is accessible to all teachers, whatever combination of language skills they possess, and contrary to the reputation of this technique as a dusty and pedantic practice, most people, students and teachers alike, not only benefit from the activity but actually find it enjoyable and personally fulfilling.

A technique of the future
In other words, the use of translation as an aid to teaching is not an outmoded technique that we should consign to the dustbin of the past. On the contrary, the use of guided translation in the ELT classroom, whether that classroom is a real-world one or a virtual one, is a valuable resource that merely needs fine-tuning and expanding to become a technique of the future.

References
Abboud, A. (2003) Lecture at University of Bonn; Qantara/ Deutsche Welle 20.03.2003

Canagarajah, A. S. (1999) *Resisting Linguistic Imperialism in English Language Teaching,* Oxford University Press

Claypole, M. (2010) *Translation and ELT,* Linguabooks/BOD

Klevberg, R. (2000) *The Role of Translation in Japanese Young Learner Classrooms,* The Language Teacher October 2000

Krashen, S. D. (1981) *Principles and Practice in Second Language Acquisition.* English Language Teaching Series, Prentice-Hall International, London

Maley, A., cited by Owen (q.v.)

Nott, D. (2005) *Translation from and into the foreign language, Guide to Good Practice for learning and teaching in Languages,* Linguistics and Area Studies

Owen, D. (2003) 'Where's the Treason in Translation?' in *HLT Magazine* Year 5, Issue 1, January 2003

Petrocchi, V. (2006) 'Translation as an Aid in Teaching English as a Second Language' in Translation Journal Vol. 10 No. 4

Snow, D. (1992) *Eight Approaches to Language Teaching,* CAL Digests, Center for Applied Linguistics, Washington DC

Context, content, COLT

How to teach Technical English

In 2009 I was invited to give a talk on teaching Technical English at the first IATET Day in Stuttgart. IATET is the recently founded International Association of Technical English Trainers and this one-day event was broadcast live on the internet to an international audience. This chapter is based on that presentation and is published here in print for the first time.

A paper presented in 2009...

Although I have been teaching Technical English at various levels for many years, it had been quite a while since I had addressed fellow teachers on this topic, so whilst preparing my presentation, I consulted my notes for a series of workshops I had held in the 1990s entitled simply 'Teaching Technical English'.

... against the background of earlier workshops

Flashback to a simpler world

Previous workshops focussed on the communicative aspects of language teaching...

In that earlier series of talks, I had stressed the importance of communication and the parallels between Technical English training and other types of ELT, and although it was only one of the aspects I had outlined at that time, part of my purpose then was to motivate teachers of Business English and General English to adapt their techniques to the teaching of Technical English by focussing on the communicative aspects of the language, or in the words of one announcement for those early talks, 'to promote teacher confidence ... by presenting the problems involved and suggesting ways of dealing with them.'

At that time I defined Technical English in the context of the ELT classroom as 'communicating in a technical context' and this approach does indeed now seem to have entered the domain of received wisdom as more and more 'communicative' Technical English books come onto the market and an increasing number of Business English teachers seek to adapt their techniques to the field of Technical English.

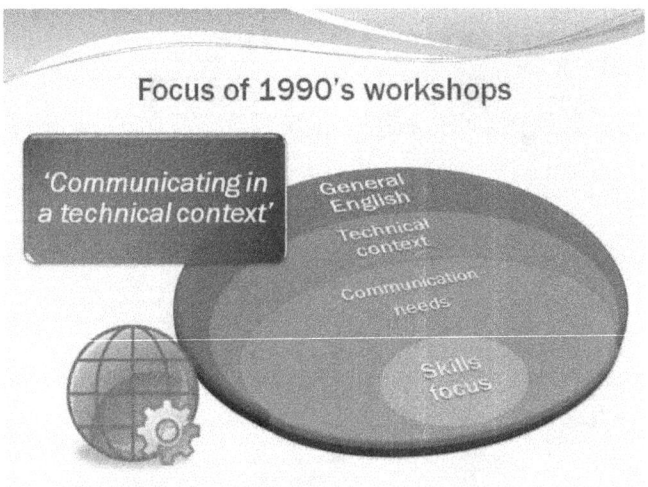

The communicative focus I had previously advocated

This view sees General English as something vague and amorphous which encompasses many fields, of which the technical domain is one. If Technical English is a subset of General English, then it follows that the student's communicative needs can be derived from areas outside the field of technology and the teacher can therefore home in on the same kind of skills taught in other language classes.

In the intervening years, however, it seems to me that what I had then intended to be nothing other than a point of departure has now become an end in itself, resulting in an over-emphasis on communication skills in the Technical English classroom. Technical English books often assume that what engineers need to do is to talk about their work, attend meetings, make telephone calls and give presentations. Language is often generalised with a focus on structural and functional elements – describing processes, using the passive, the language of graphs and charts, that kind of thing. My contention here is that while this communication-oriented approach is easy for the non-specialist language teacher, it does not necessarily deliver what the students really want.

... but times have changed.

Students will generally go along with a communicative approach, not because it is the right one, but because it has now become the norm and because on the whole they are not aware that there is an alternative; indeed, if all the courses available to them are designed in this way, then they have no alternatives to choose from. After all, from an engineering student's point of view, any Technical English course is probably better than a General English one. But if the students really needed to learn how to converse and to describe processes – if the focus were on fluency rather than accuracy – they would be better off in a General English course. And if they really needed to make phone calls, present facts and figures and enter into negotiations, they would have signed up for Business English.

Technical English learners can be flexible...

.. but their needs are not the same as those of Business English students.

Furthermore, times have changed. Busy professionals no longer see Business English as something special; for many adult learners, it has become the norm. Consequently, there is a growing need to look more closely at the learners' specific requirements and develop teaching strategies to match.

Methodology of Technical English under attack

We must distinguish between different types of ELT...

Now, I'm all in favour of pedagogical synergy and the intelligent transfer of techniques and methodologies, but it seems to me that there has recently been a strong tendency to import ideas and methods which work well when teaching General or Business English, and which require only a marginal degree of specialisation on the part of the teacher, or from other forms of ESP (English for Special Purposes) such as legal or medical, which are not only specialised in content but also associated with very specific professions and skill sets.

CLIL (content and language integrated teaching) is a fairly recent development which has no specific skills focus, but this is a notion which is embedded in state school systems and, like Academic English, is frequently syllabus-bound and exam-oriented. None of this applies to the majority of Technical English teaching situations. In other words, all these forms of ELT make assumptions about the learner profile which do not match that of the typical student of Technical English. From a teacher's point of view, the teaching of Technical English requires a different approach. Above all, **we can not differentiate Technical English courses from other variants of ELT by doing the same thing.**

Technical English is a subset of ESP with a strong focus on content (technology and engineering). It is not industry-specific, since engineers work in many industries and many sectors. A topic such as electrical engineering, mechatronics or fluid dynamics is defined by the subject matter and not by any specific application or particular profession. End-users of the target language are defined by the knowledge they need to acquire and the language they need to learn, which places a particular emphasis on understanding a wide range of content within their subject area rather than perfecting a set of universal linguistic skills. The teacher therefore needs to focus on the specific language to be learned by ensuring that the content is truly relevant.

... and take the real needs of the learners into account.

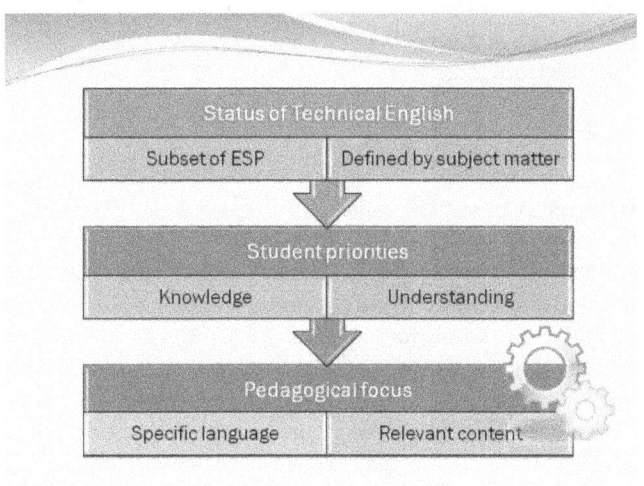

Differentiation of Technical English

Equally crucial are the factors that motivate the learners. Since the target group is not associated with any specific profession – the students may be design engineers, car mechanics, toolmakers or materials experts and may work in R & D, production or sales and so on – they are connected only by the areas of language they need to learn. We can not, therefore, make assumptions about the skills they may need for their work, except that there is usually a strong need to perform passive tasks such as reading,

Learners of Technical English are united by their language needs, not their professions.

understanding and extracting information. Often, the use they put these passive skills to lies outside the scope of the classroom, as indeed does much of their daily work.

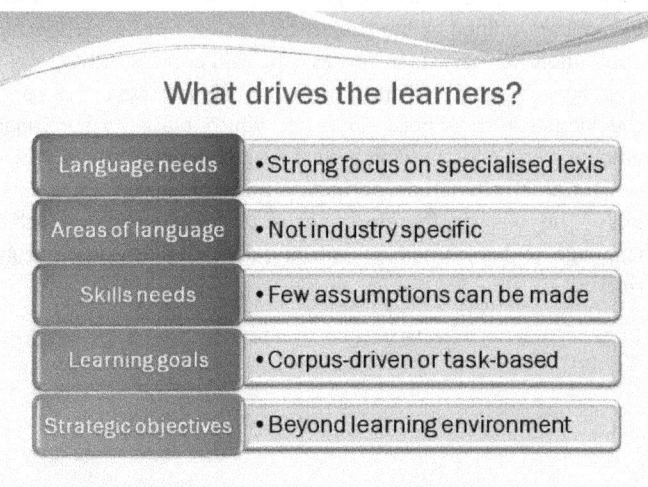

The factors that drive the learners

Technical English courses should be based on content.

From the foregoing, it follows that Technical English courses should ideally focus on content rather than on skills. It is not uncommon, however, for Technical English courses to sacrifice depth of content in favour of a strong focus on communicative ability. Alternatively, a well-meaning search for authentic materials can result in materials being used which are not really suitable for the classroom or, in the case of engineering textbooks, may even challenge the teacher's own knowledge base, and as we have seen, transferring methods from other areas may make false assumptions about the both teacher and student.

CONTROVERSIES IN ELT

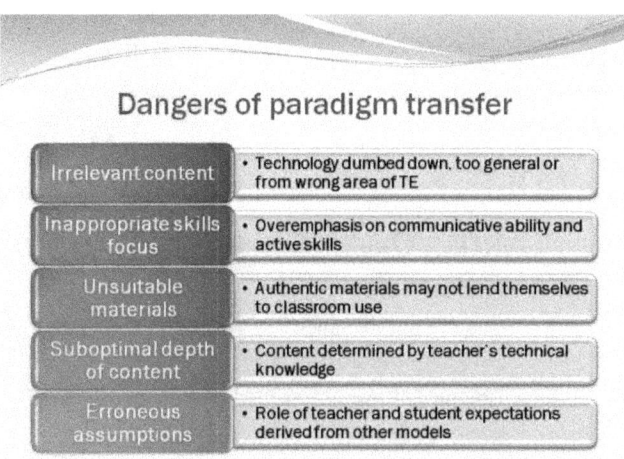

The dangers of transferring inappropriate paradigms

In the Technical English sector, there is therefore a need for a methodological approach which places greater emphasis on subject matter and authentic, relevant materials, and it is for the purpose of crystallising this concept that I have created the acronym 'COLT'.

The first two letters of the acronym clearly indicate that this is a content-oriented (CO) approach to classroom practice. The 'L' stands for 'language' because the prime objective is to teach the language itself rather than language-related skills, and this language must be of specific interest to the target group, otherwise the whole exercise will be pretty futile. In terms of Technical English, typical areas include: mechanical and electrical engineering, automotive technologies, mechatronics, surface finishing, materials-related topics (metals, ceramics, chemicals, wood, paper) and process-specific subjects such as manufacturing, testing, job control, quality assurance, R & D, etc.

Why 'COLT' and what it really means

Introducing a new paradigm

COLT
- CONTENT-ORIENTED LANGUAGE TEACHING

- Focus on:
  - Content before skills
  - Language before function
  - Teaching strategies before learning activities

Introducing the COLT paradigm

In the COLT paradigm, the teacher is not a skills coach...

Obviously, the 'T' stands for 'teaching', but this is not merely an arbitrary descriptor; indeed it is a key indicator of the underlying philosophy. In General and Business English, many language learning activities are student-centred; they focus on what the learner does, e.g. homework assignments, self-study, group work, peer-group learning, taking part in discussions, using reference works, reading, listening etc. In these activities, the learner takes pride of place. After all, **a student can learn without a teacher, but a teacher can not teach without a learner.** Most teachers therefore strive to adopt a student-centred approach. However, in the teaching of Technical English to adults, much of what the student does (e.g. how much time any given student spends on homework assignments or actively taking part in class discussions) is either beyond the control of the teacher or promotes language skills which fall under the categories of General English or communication skills. To a large extent, the teacher is a facilitator of learning, rather than a provider of knowledge or a skills coach.

... but a facilitator of learning.

The COLT approach focuses on what the teacher does to promote learning, rather than on the skills the student acquires through this teaching. In essence, it is a teacher-centred approach. COLT therefore entails developing teaching (rather than learning) strategies which are designed to communicate or facilitate content-relevant language to learners. COLT is a dynamic and active process. It puts **content before skills, language before function** and **teaching strategies before learning activities.**

COLT is a teacher-centred approach.

So what sort of methodology is appropriate for COLT? In the COLT model, the content is determined by the student profile and their learning goals. This helps us to define the language input for any given lesson, carefully selecting authentic source material which matches the students' level and their language needs. We use a kind of Occam's razor to eliminate anything that is not actually relevant and take a task-based approach to ensure that the language is of practical value. Unlike some other forms of ELT, we pay more attention to written than to oral interaction and promote passive skills rather than active language production.

Source material should be carefully selected…

Ideally, this takes place in a dynamic environment in which methods are constantly being adapted to suit the teacher/student model and which freely take advantage of peer group teaching, spontaneous student input, bilingual methodologies, discussions in the students' native language, increased teacher talking time and even more quiet time than you might find in other classes as students work independently on new content input.

… and subjected to constant revision.

Language learning in a dynamic environment

Methodology of COLT

- Student objectives determine content
- Content determines language input
- Carefully selected authentic source material
- Relevancy check
- Task-based
- Focus on written rather than oral skills
- Focus on passive rather than active skills
- Dynamic teaching-learning cycle

Methodology of COLT

A practical example...

The following example is from an in-company course held in Germany. The teacher has established in advance that the students work in the field of electroplating. The class consists of development engineers, sales staff and hot line personnel. A classic mistake would be to teach them all how to handle hot line calls in general, leaving them to discover the technical language for themselves and simultaneously wasting the time of the non-hot line staff.

... based on an in-company course.

Instead, we take a content-based approach and locate some relevant input material. We have identified the area of electroplating as being of prime interest to our students and have selected a relevant item of equipment which will enable us to focus on the principles of electrolysis as well as the programming and operation of an electroforming machine. Since some of the students are development engineers, we also wish to incorporate the language of troubleshooting within this context.

Classroom example

Subject area: electroplating
- Electroforming machine
- Principles of electrolysis
- Programming
- Operation
- Troubleshooting

COLT *in practice – a classroom example*

In preparing this lesson, we do not search for material that is easy to teach, but for content that is truly relevant. We are going to start the lesson by playing a video highlighting the target technology.

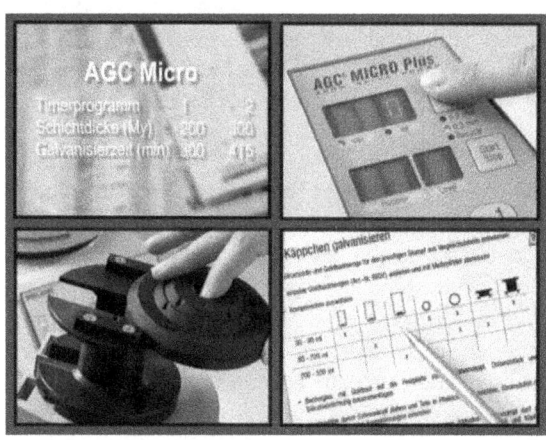

Screenshots *from the introductory video*

In this example, neither the soundtrack nor the captions shown in the video are in English, since the video was made for the company's German-speaking clientele. This should not deter us from using it, since in the introductory phase of the lesson, it is better to present the right content in the student's own language than the wrong content in English. In fact, it isn't even necessary for the teacher to understand the language used in the video, as long as the students do. The reason for this will become apparent as I outline the lesson plan below.

Authentic input material...

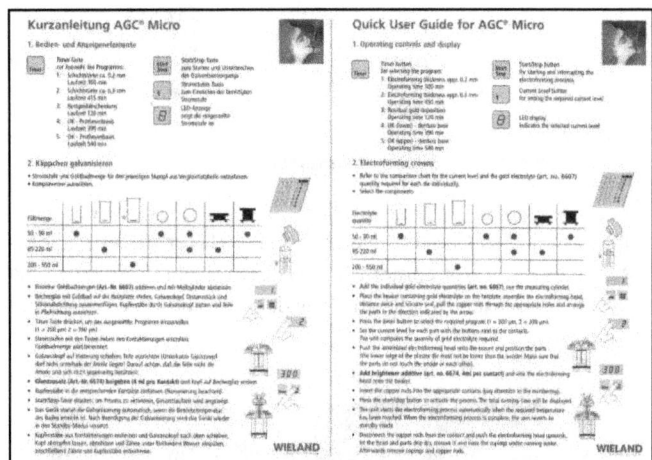

Raw material for this lesson: Quick User Guide in two languages

... does not always have to be in English.

Although in this instance we do not have access to video material in English, what we do have is a Quick User Guide in both the students' language and in English. By using the video in the start-up phase of the lesson, we have established that the content is understood and can now concentrate on the language. The illustration below shows how the Quick User Guide can be transformed into classroom material. And at this stage, the teacher simply uses whatever works, adapting the material and designing tasks to ensure that learning takes place. To be quite honest, as long as you are teaching the right thing, it hardly matters **how** you do it. It is **what** you teach that counts (cf. p. 22).

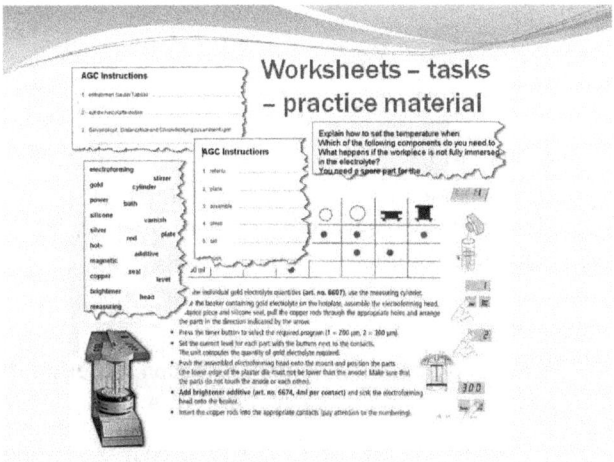

Worksheets prepared from in-house material

One of the factors that distinguish this model from others is the greater exploitation of the students' own language in the classroom. In the COLT model, there is no taboo on using L1 in class, so explanations and discussions in L1, translation work, bilingual materials and code-switching exercises can all be exploited. L1 also plays a stronger part in the preparation phase, where the teacher's knowledge of the parallels and differences between the source and target languages is an important factor in the selection and development of teaching materials.

Worksheets must be highly relevant.

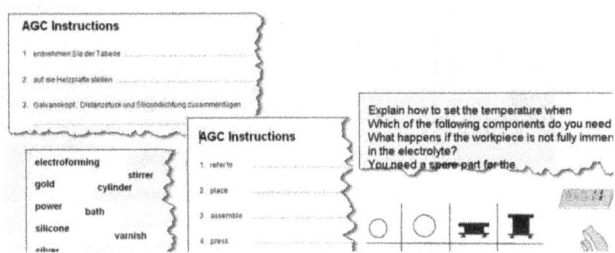

Worksheets – detail

Use of L1 in COLT

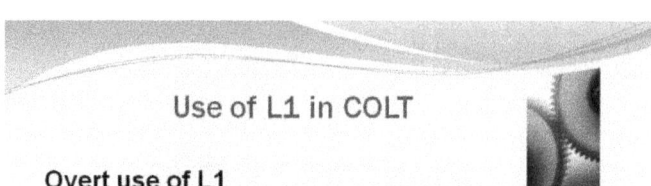

Overt use of L1
- Explanations, discussions in students' mother tongue, translation work, bilingual materials, code-switching exercises, input materials

There are many ways to exploit the students' native language.

Covert use of L1
- Lesson preparation, content selection, materials development, comparative linguistics

Use of the students' native language in the COLT model

A platform for practising relevant skills.

In addition to vocabulary expansion, the focus on content provides a platform for practising relevant skills such as understanding documentation, discussing specific content, describing processes, drafting documentation and summarising, to name but a few.

The author presenting the COLT approach to a worldwide audience...

In addition to vocabulary expansion, the focus on content provides a platform for practising relevant skills such as:

- Understanding documentation
- Discussing specific content
- Describing processes
- Drafting documentation
- Summarising

Focus on content-related skills

COLT therefore makes relevant content the point of departure for each lesson. Teaching the right content will also promote the appropriate skills. Wherever possible, teachers should use authentic content, whatever the source. In other words, if you find that the materials you are using don't include the right content, you need to go where the content is, to research the topic in English and if possible in the students' L1 as well. And when it comes to detailed classroom techniques, you use only those methods that actually work with your particular group of students.

The teacher must research the topic and its language.

... and taking questions.

99

Pedagogical principles

Teaching the right content will promote the appropriate **SKILLS**.

Make relevant **CONTENT** the point of departure for each lesson.

Where possible, use **AUTHENTIC** content, whatever the source.

If existing materials don't include the content you need, **GO WHERE THE CONTENT IS**.

RESEARCH the topic in English and in the students' language.

Use only teaching methods which **ACTUALLY SUIT** the teacher/student pattern.

Pedagogical principles

Teaching the wrong content can not be effective...

The COLT paradigm is therefore a teacher-centred approach. It focuses on language content rather than on usage and whilst it does not ignore communication skills, it puts learner-specific content first, ensuring that the skills practised are relevant to the real needs of the student.

... therefore the content must be right.

In other words, if the content is wrong (e.g. because the teacher uses what is available or easy to teach etc.), relevant learning cannot take place. **If the content is right, teaching will be relevant and learning may just take place.**

Summary

The COLT paradigm

- is a teacher-centred approach
- focuses on language content rather than usage
- does not ignore communication skills, but puts learner-specific content first, ensuring that the skills practised are relevant to the real needs of the student

Summary of the COLT paradigm

As I write this in early 2010, the COLT paradigm has attracted the interest of industry and further presentations and articles are planned. Time permitting, the latest information on this topic will be posted online at www.mauriceclaypole.com/colt.

Source of further information

The circles of your mind

Introducing word set maps

Nowadays, mind maps are quite frequently used as a method of organising vocabulary and visualising contributions during meetings, brainstorming sessions and language classes. Indeed, I frequently use a similar technique in my own English classes, but with one significant difference: I use circles, ellipses and sometimes rather amorphous shapes to indicate the conceptual relationship between words. Since I currently teach English in a German-speaking environment, I also make frequent use of bilingual examples to indicate the overlaps and interfaces between the two languages. This chapter therefore makes reference to some English/German correlations, but knowledge of German is not really necessary in order to follow the examples given.

Word set maps show how the meanings of words overlap.

To describe these graphical representations, I have coined the term 'word set maps.' To illustrate how these work, let us take a fairly simple abstract concept, that of *happiness*. The procedure for creating word set maps then goes something like this:

First we define the limits of the original notion (fig. 1).

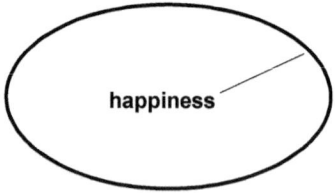

Fig. 1

Then we add related concepts or supposed synonyms, placing each new addition according to our assessment of how well the concept overlaps (intersects) with the existing ones (fig. 2).

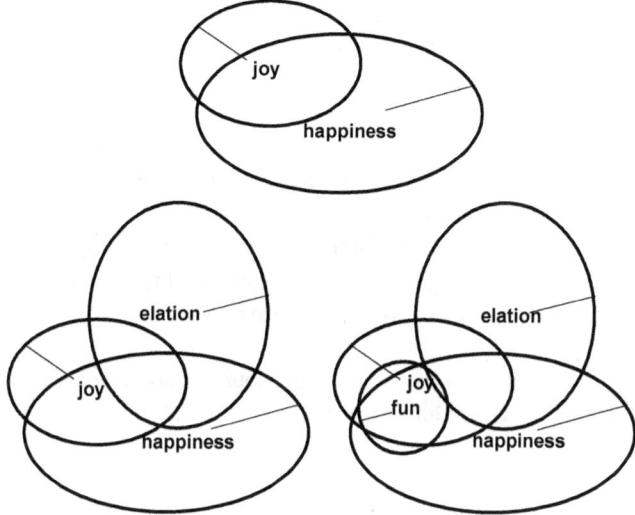

Fig. 2

Eventually, a more complex picture is built up and the areas under study can be shaded in or labelled (fig. 3).

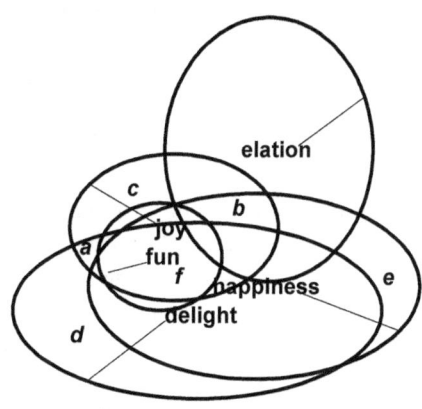

Fig. 3

This results in a kind of visual thesaurus mapping out the sets of meanings covered by the words under study. The example above is by no means complete, but it serves as a graphic illustration of the principle that whilst the concepts depicted are all related, their degree of common usage varies considerably. In some situations, two or more of them may be interchangeable, e.g.

It was a joy/delight to watch the children play.

This is indicated by the intersecting areas of the map, in this case area *a*, which gives us the set {joy;delight}. Below I have indicated the respective set map area in parentheses.

One notes that in this example the source word *happiness* falls outside the area of intersection, since it cannot be meaningfully substituted, whereas other contexts permit this:

His delight/joy/happiness/elation at hearing the news was so great...(b)

In other instances, idiomatic usage may not allow any alternatives, as for example in

Our choice of words is often more dependent on idiom and precedent than on meaning.

She leapt for joy when she received the news. (c)

They were swept into transports of delight. (d)

The pursuit of happiness is man's highest goal. (e)

It very quickly becomes evident that our instinctive lexical choice is often determined more by idiom and precedent than by any clear distinction in meaning, but it is also important to bear in mind that intersections indicate common usage patterns within a broad semantic range, not necessarily areas of identical meaning:

Although she was rich, there was no fun/joy/happiness in her life. (f)

However, once we have produced a map based on actual examples of usage and our general semantic perceptions, we can draw on it to support a variety of postulates along the lines:

> *happiness* ∉ *fun*

and

> *happiness* ⊄ *fun*

but

> *happiness* ∪ *fun* ⊆ *joy*

If a specific instance stands the test of further examples, then we have gained a new insight into the way language works; if not, we go back and modify the map by shifting, expanding or contracting the various sets.

Explanation of symbols			
⊂	is a subset of	⊇	includes or is equal to
⊆	is a subset of or equal to	∪	combined with
⊄	is not a subset of	∩	intersects
∈	is an element of	→	leads to
∉	is not an element of	←	derives from
⊃	includes	∴	therefore

At this point, set maps (like mind maps) seem to take over and become a joy(!) in themselves, a method of searching our own thoughts and examining our linguistic perceptions. I very much doubt if two people given the same set of basic lexical items would produce even remotely similar maps. However, to use set maps in the classroom they must be kept fairly simple, i.e. the terminology depicted must be selected carefully, even if the maps are drawn spontaneously. (I have never yet prepared such a map beforehand, although I always have a clear idea before starting a lesson of where the technique is going to take me,

Set maps represent a personal interpretation.

since I know which semantic problems I intend to highlight. And as in my case, I am teaching in a situation in which I can also draw on the students' L1, this gives me the additional option of creating bilingual set maps, which is where the principle really comes into its own. The shapes used are quite arbitrary; in the illustrations below I have used different geometric figures to distinguish between English and German lexical items. In practice I mostly use amoebic forms, stretching them as I please to achieve the required overlaps.

Bilingual set maps...

Since my purpose in the classroom (teaching new vocabulary, or more frequently correcting misconceptions arising through false correlation with L1) is less exploratory, the result is not an exploding fractal-like map of terminology, but a somewhat more introspective depiction of semantic relationships illustrating the sets to which related L2 words belong. The result often comes as a surprise to students, but is invariably greeted with understanding. And if we superimpose a supposed synonym in L1 we often get at the root of many mistranslations and misconceptions. For example, any native German speaker who might think that *happiness* is the English word for *Glück* should consider first the L1 set map shown in fig. 4.

... reveal the source of many mistranslations.

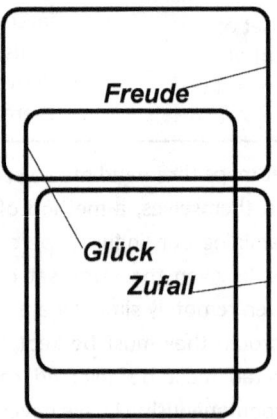

Fig. 4

The sheer size of the correlation between *Glück* and *Zufall* should be a warning to any learner, especially in view of the fact that no equivalent for *Zufall* (such as *chance* or *coincidence*) would occur in the corresponding English set map.[16] If we added such a word there would be no intersection with existing sets. In other words, the set

Zufall ∩ *Glück*

does not exist as a concept in English, although

Freude ∩ *Glück*

does.

This means that we can attempt cross-language definitions of *happiness* and *Glück*:

happiness = Glück / Zufall

Glück ∪ Freude = happiness

In a teaching situation, the main purpose of depicting such relationships in graphical form is to impress upon learners that the equals sign alone is not only an inadequate method of correlation representation; it is often misleading. In my experience, occasional word set maps used as a visual aid can succeed where other forms of notation, or lengthy explanations, may fail. When learners are able to appreciate that words are only vague representations of a variety of concepts in L1, then they are no longer surprised to find a divergent pattern in L2. And here I must emphasise that it is primarily a question of awareness, not

Word set maps help to improve the learner's awareness of meaning.

---

[16] At least not in modern English. Etymologically, *happiness* is cognate with the verb *happen* and hence is related to other notions of randomness such as *happenchance*. Strictly speaking, *happiness* is something that either happens, or does not, as the case may be. Modern German has retained this notion; English has not.

107

of notation, one of principle rather than of detail. In the classroom, I am satisfied if learners replace their classical notation:

$$happiness = Glück$$

with something like

$$happiness \subset Glück$$

since there are more disparate items classifiable by the German term than by the English one. Leaving the classroom for a moment, however, one could argue that there are other uses of *happiness* which are outside the scope of *Glück*, so I would also accept:

$$Glück \supseteq happiness$$

although it would be more accurate to surmise that both terms are elements of a theoretical superset from which each derive certain semantic characteristics:

$$Glück \in X$$

$$happiness \in X$$

$$\therefore \{Glück; happiness\} = X$$

but the elements of the superset are also word sets in their own right:

$$Glück \subset X$$

$$happiness \subset X$$

$$\therefore Glück \cup happiness = X$$

from which a set of the deficiency of one set over the other can be derived:

$$Y = happiness / Glück$$

In other words, Y is an area of non-intersection between the two sets, an indication (as is evident from the graphical representation) that the superset of all notions encompassed by the map is greater than the original point of departure (*happiness*). We can therefore postulate sets of emotions which exist, but for which there are no known words:

Some meanings have no words.

$$X_1 = \{satisfaction; contentment; happiness; joy; delight; bliss; ecstasy; ...\}$$

$$X_2 = \{Zufriedenheit; Spaß; Glück; Freude; Entzückung; Wonne; ...\}$$

$$Y_1 = \{Zufall; Möglichkeit; Chance; Gelegenheit; ...\}$$

$$Z_1 = \{X_1; X_2\} (...)$$

Of course, chaos ensues when we superimpose even the simplest of L2 set maps on their L1 counterparts, but then this should not be surprising since language is chaotic[17] by nature. As a result, adding further near synonyms to a map in progress makes the whole picture grow in a veritable journey of discovery (fig. 5).

Adding the L2 set map to the L1 map results in a chaotic picture.

---

[17] Scientifically speaking, chaos is not a random quality, but is a deterministic notion, being generated by fixed rules which, however, contain so many uncertainties that results are unpredictable (see next chapter).

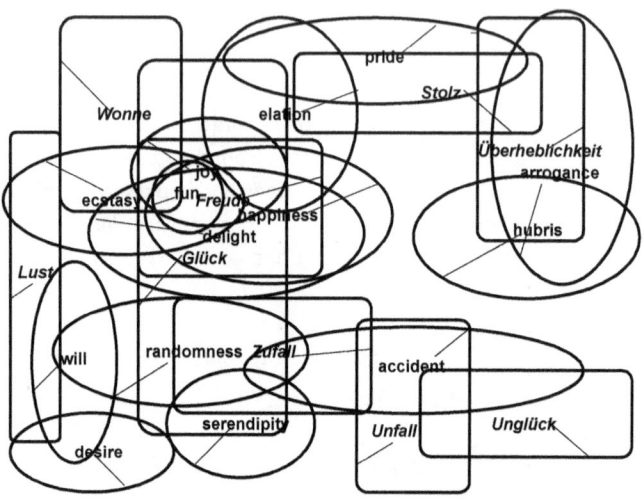

Fig. 5

One can add to the map at will, but a great deal of attention is necessary to ensure that only plausible intersections occur and in order to achieve a modicum of completeness. In this instance, our search has taken us from *happiness* and *Glück* to words one may not have thought of as having common uses, such as *arrogance* (via *delight* → *elation* → *pride* → *Stolz* → *Überheblichkeit*) and even *Unglück* (via *Zufall* → *accident* → *Unfall*).

You don't really discover your own language until you teach it.

At this point, the borderline between the use of these maps as a teaching aid and as a method for creative discovery seems to have been well and truly crossed, and why indeed should these applications be regarded as mutual exclusives? As I am sure all language teachers would agree: **you don't really find out about your own language, let alone a foreign one, until you teach it.**

Chaos and dynamism in language teaching

The birth of the fractal approach

Introduction

Rather than seeking simple solutions to complex problems, language teachers might do well to look beyond the confines of conventional language teaching to the lessons learned by other scientific disciplines. The fractal approach sees language as a dynamic process characterised by self-organisation, self-similarity and chaotic determination. Once taken on board, this approach can change the way you view language and radically affect your teaching.

The fractal approach sees language as a dynamic process.

Background

My interest in the fascinating world of fractal forms goes back to the 1980's and was heightened in 1992 when I was asked on behalf of Springer-Verlag to translate a book on business process engineering by the then head of the Fraunhofer Institute for Manufacturing Engineering and Automation, Professor Hans-Jürgen Warnecke. My English translation appeared in 1993 under the title *The Fractal Company – A Revolution in Corporate Culture*. Whilst working on the manuscript, I came to the conclusion that the insights Warnecke had transferred from fractal geometry to modern industrial corporations were even more universal than was often assumed, and one of the areas where I began to identify fractals was in the field of languages and language teaching. I first introduced the notion of the **fractality of language** and the **dynamic** (or **fractal**) **approach to language teaching** in a series of lectures given between 1999 and 2002, but the content has not previously been available in print. Now, however, these ideas are set out in detail in *The Fractal Approach to Teaching English as a Foreign Language Teaching* (2010, ISBN 978-3-8391-3382-8) and summarised here.

Introducing fractals into the field of language study and coining the term 'fractality'

A real-world phenomenon

Most approaches to ELT treat language as an artificial construct rather than as a real world phenomenon. The reasons for this are almost lost in history. They date back to the time when the only 'foreign' languages to be formally taught in Europe were Latin and Greek. And these were taught not as living languages of day-to-day use by native speakers, but as a vehicle for the study of religious and literary texts and as a mental discipline. Language was taught not as a real world system but as an artificial construct consisting of vocabulary as the building blocks of language and grammar as the mortar that holds the bricks together and shapes the whole into the required form. Even the progression through audio-lingual, functional-notional, communicative and lexical approaches has done little to shake this ideology. This applies not only to the content and the language structures we select for teaching, but also to the way we teach and the way we define our role as teachers. Teaching and learning a language incorporates skills and knowledge from all areas of human activity and interaction, not only from commerce and industry, but from the arts and the humanities, from psychology and physiology, from medicine and the natural sciences, from physics, chemistry and even mathematics.

> *The classical view sees language as an artificial construct consisting blocks of vocabulary held together by the mortar of grammar.*

The theory

Let me illustrate the theory with an example from daily life. There are few things that affect our lives more than the weather, and life would be so much simpler if we knew for sure what tomorrow's weather would be like. And yet, despite the massive amount of computing power available to meteorological centres, it is still impossible to predict the weather with the degree of accuracy we would like. Why is this so? Why are changes in weather patterns so difficult to predict? Why do we so often watch the nice man or woman on television forecast sunshine and then take an umbrella anyway, just in case? The answer is that the weather not only changes, but that it changes in a dynamic way as seemingly insignificant factors are fed back into a loop of cause and effect in which the magnitude of the effects

> *We cannot reliably predict the weather...*

> *... because it changes in a dynamic way.*

bears no relation to that of the input values, a phenomenon which frequently produces unexpected results (fig. 1).

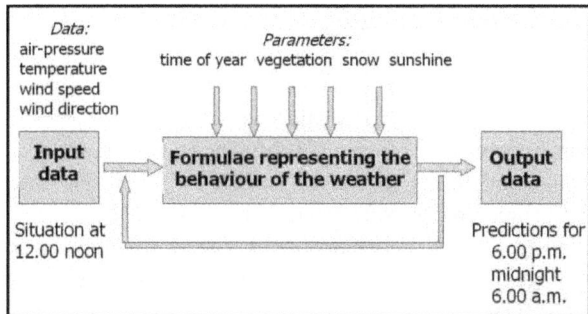

Fig. 1 *Weather feedback cycle as an iterative system*

Teachers of Business English in particular will recognise parallels here to the way the stock market operates or the influence of external factors on commodities, interest rates and real estate prices. Values not only change; they change in a dynamic way. Dynamism is more than just change. And chaos is more than just dynamism. Dynamic systems such as the weather or the stock market are iterative; they are subject to repeated changes in their initial states, but this in itself would not matter much if small changes in the input values resulted in small changes in the output values. Unfortunately, this is not the case. When we are looking at weather systems, extremely small variations in the initial states or values can result in massive variations in the output results. This gives rise to the so-called butterfly effect: this oft-cited, albeit probably apocryphal example asserts that if a butterfly flaps its wings in South America it can result in a hurricane in Asia. This is the state that we refer to as 'chaos' and this is what we mean when we say that the weather is a 'chaotic' system. It not only changes through dynamic iteration, but the changes are of such a nature that they defy prediction. Such systems are often referred to as 'complex systems'. And I would argue that language, too, is a complex or chaotic system.

Dynamism is more than change...

... and chaos is more than dynamism.

Changes through dynamic iteration are chaotic and defy prediction.

Language is subject to ongoing change in a feedback loop.

Like other dynamic systems, the language we use is subject to ongoing change in a feedback cycle in which results can rarely be predicted. This applies both to syntactic structures and to the meaning of individual utterances. Each time a word or expression is used, it acquires a new valence as a result of external factors such as the context in which it was uttered, the intention of the speaker and the medium in which it was used (fig. 2). A simple example would be the associations created by a successful marketing slogan like 'Where do you want to go today?' (IBM) 'Reach out and touch someone.' (AT&T), or a comedy catch phrase ('Computer says No.' (David Walliams), 'Am I bovvered?' (Catherine Tate), but this phenomenon applies to every use of the language and is the generating force behind all forms of peer group discourse from Cockney slang and Hinglish to financial jargon, political obfuscation and legalese.

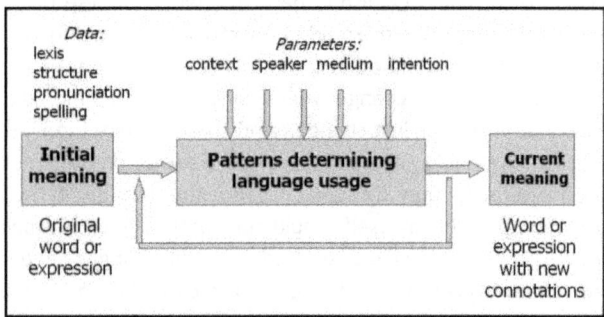

Fig. 2 *The effect of iteration on meaning*

The fractal paradigm

A fractal form manifests self-organisation, self-similarity and dynamism.

Nowhere is this iterative pattern more dramatically present than in the domain of fractal imaging. Essentially, a fractal is nothing more than a geometric form. Unlike the shapes of Euclidean geometry, however, fractals exhibit three main characteristics: self-organisation, self-similarity and dynamism. Fractals are generated by iteration, resulting in a chaotic pattern resembling those found in nature. The main difference between a simple form such as a circle and a fractal lies in the detail. Whereas zooming in on a circle reveals nothing new, inspecting a fractal in detail reveals ever greater degrees of sophistication. In a manner akin to putting a leaf or an insect's leg under a microscope, the closer you look at it, the more fascinating it becomes. Like the circle and the sphere, the fractal is a mathematical construct, but unlike the perfect sphere, it is a dynamic form that can be found in the real world. In his book, *Fractals Everywhere*, the mathematician, Michael Barnsley makes the following observation:

Zooming in on a fractal reveals increasing detail.

> 'Fractal geometry will make you see everything differently... You risk the loss of your childhood vision of clouds, forests, galaxies, leaves, feathers, flowers, rocks, mountains, torrents of water, carpets, bricks, and much else besides. Never again will your interpretation of these things be quite the same.'
>
> **Barnsley (1988)**

And never again, I would add, will your view of language be quite the same.

The most commonly cited example of a fractal is the Mandelbrot set. The formula that generates it is deceptively simple but produces fantastic results. A graphical extrapolation of the values of c for which the orbit of 0 under iteration of

A 'simple' fractal

$$\{z_{n+1} = z_n^2 + c\}$$

remains bounded produces a myriad of increasingly complex images (fig. 3).

Fig. 3 Zooming in on the Mandelbrot set (top left) reveals forms of increasing complexity (bottom left and left-hand images)

Fractal forms resemble natural shapes.

More strikingly, fractal forms are uncannily similar to the shapes we find in nature. From the leaves on a tree to whole continents, from the subatomic forms of quantum mechanics to whirling galaxies, the fractality of the natural world is ever-present.

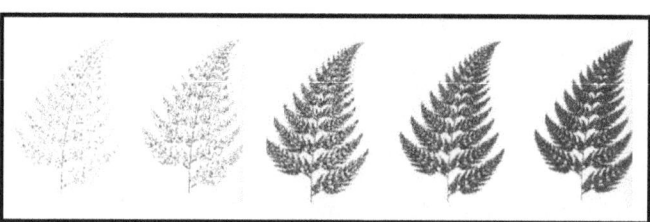

Fig. 4 Computer-generated fractal fern

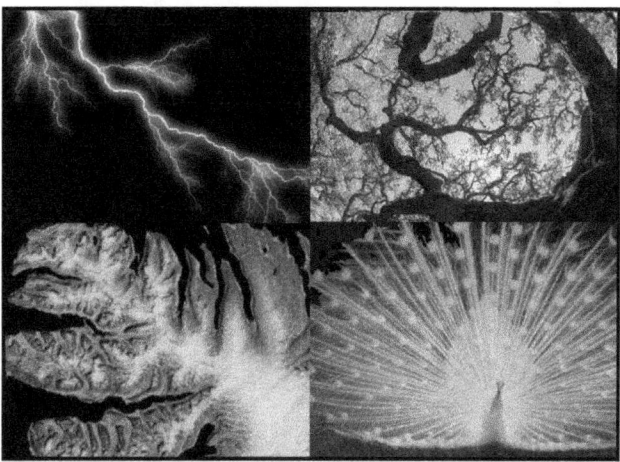

Fig. 5 Fractal forms in nature: lightning, trees, fjords, peacock feathers

Consequences for ELT

The implications of this for our work as language teachers may not at first be obvious, but I believe that they are far-reaching. The basic tenet of this paradigm is that human language mirrors certain forms found in nature. By implication, this favours a goal-oriented method of teaching combined with a holistic view of language acquisition. In the classroom situation, this entails an even greater use of authentic material than is currently practised, accompanied by an adjustment of the expectations of both teacher and student. The fundamental principles can be expressed quite simply:

Language mirrors natural forms and exhibits fractal characteristics.

- Human language is a self-organising, self-similar, dynamic system.
- It is a real world phenomenon.
- It is not governed by simple rules but driven by an ongoing, iterative process of interaction and feedback.
- English usage obeys a set of 'laws', but these are complex in nature and often defy prediction.

Grammatical and lexical approaches cannot work in a dynamic system.

The dynamic nature of language is one of the reasons for the ultimate failure of the grammatical and lexical approaches and reveals key inconsistencies in other formalised notions such as communicative and task-based teaching. Simple grammatical rules representing a static system are effective but misleading from beginner to intermediate level. At these levels, they tend to work until you close the course book, but they totally run out of steam when students progress beyond the stage of CEFR B2. You only need to open any so-called advanced course book to find examples of this. 'Cleft sentences' and 'non-defining relative clauses' are two of my favourite examples of this kind of aberration. Beyond B2, the grammar content of conventional course material usually becomes more **complicated** (e.g. learning the forms of the present perfect continuous or categorising different kinds of conditionals), but it is not actually more advanced and it is not **complex**, since even complicated oversimplifications represent a static rather than a dynamic system.

For similar reasons, attempts to implement the lexical approach at levels below B2 generally fail because the concept itself is restrictive and by definition excludes whole areas of language use from the field of study. Over-formalisation of this kind treats language not as a real world system but as an artificial construct. We put in the vocabulary, apply grammar and turn the handle – and out comes our target language. The required input produces the required output.

By using language, we change it.

The dynamic model, however, recognizes that by using the language, we change it. Once you have used a word or a phrase in a new context, it acquires associations and meanings it did not have before. Sometimes these changes are obvious. Simple expressions such as 'war' and 'terror' and any combination of these now have meanings – or at least different connotations and more wide-ranging associations – than they had just a few years ago, whilst in financial circles, the mere mention of terms such as 'sub-prime', 'crunch', 'Iceland' and 'banker' can send shivers through the spine. In many real-life situations, non-grammatical utterances far outweigh those that obey clear sets of rules: A'o / she's good people / got lag? get prim hog buster / JFK afk / PM under fire in peers storm / the most unkindest cut / tomorrow snow is *drifting across… / say me what you want / eat my chuddies, innit?* etc. whilst brand new utterances, too, can be pre-charged with association and innuendo: *The future's bright, but it ain't orange / the only gay in the company / disconnecting people / hell hath no jury* etc. Without this almost infinite degree of flexibility and allusion, there would be no humour, no poetry, no creative marketing and no linguistic innovation.

Classroom implications

Language is therefore chaotic; it consists almost entirely of shifting associations, and by teaching a language, you change it too, since you are not only interacting with learners but are changing their perception of the language, and in some cases, by teaching the language, you also modify your own perception of it. The task of teachers and course designers is therefore not to create artificial order for classroom purposes, but to prepare students for dealing with the chaos of real-world language. However, it is not necessary for the students to be able to produce the same range of language as they can understand. Not even native speakers can do this. This disparity between active and passive skills should be seen as an opportunity for exploration rather than as a factor which limits our selection of content. As I have indicated in previous chapters, it is of paramount importance to re-examine not only **how** we teach but **what** we teach, and I make no apologies for repeating this advice here.

By teaching a language, we change it.

Teachers and students must recognise the dramatic power of the context on the content and break with the notion that words and expressions have fixed meanings and that artificial constructs such as grammatical rules can be relied upon. Terms such as 'present tense', 'past tense' and 'future tense' should – if they are used at all – be recognised for what they are: arbitrary descriptors which do not reflect the way these forms are actually used. In the classroom, fluency training and confidence-building exercises may be preferable to communicating new knowledge through formal teaching. Advanced courses should not be designed to provide students with more complicated language structures nor

Words have no meanings without context.

Grammar rules can not be relied on.

to strive for perfection by eliminating perceived 'errors', but should equip students to tackle the chaos of real world language, in which meanings shift, rules either do not exist or are disregarded, and in which, very often, there are no right answers but a range of possible answers, albeit some more probable than others. Ideally, students should be made aware of the tremendous variety inherent in the English language. A language spoken by over one and a half billion people from hundreds of different countries, cultures and backgrounds does not fit easily into the straightjacket of a static system. The first consequence of this is that more attention should be paid to the passive skills required for dealing with a vast number of rapidly changing lexical sets, culturally-dominated contexts, varying intonation patterns and ethnic accents. In a wired world, students of English are more than ever before in a position to reach out beyond the course book and beyond the classroom, and what they need is guidance on how best to benefit from this experience.

Very often, there is no right answer.

A language spoken by one and a half billion people worldwide cannot fit into a static system.

At elementary level, students are satisfied if they can communicate fluently with their teacher and their peer group in the classroom. But as their own language production improves, an overdependence on a single static model can leave them fluent in one language set and deaf to the rest. How often do travellers complain that they can always get their message across and seem to understand everything that is said to them directly in negotiations but are clueless when they try to eavesdrop at what is being said at the next table in a restaurant?

Students should therefore be made aware at as early a stage as possible that the language model they adopt for active practice in the classroom, however excellent it may be, is not the only one, but is merely one probability instance in a dynamic process.

Learners should be exposed to a wide variety of form, meaning and pronunciation.

The best way to really help our learners prepare for the real world is to expose them to a wide variety of language forms, shades of meaning and pronunciation models at an early stage in their learning careers and to teach them to differentiate between the model they are required to emulate and those they should be able to understand but need not try to copy.

One further implication is that we should re-examine not only **what** we teach, but **when** we teach it. In elementary courses, for example, there is no objective reason to teach the present tense before we teach the past. And as students progress to advanced level, we should not be exposing them to ever more complicated grammatical structures but to the wealth of allusions and often non-formulaic structures of everyday speech. And above all, the language they learn should be firmly placed in a memorable context. In the real world, we are surrounded not by static systems with fixed rules but by chaos and uncertainty. And it is important to remember that as illustrated by the butterfly effect, the changes themselves do not need to be major ones in order to have a dramatic impact.

Language is best learned in a memorable context.

The fractal approach is just that. It is an approach, not a methodology; it is an attitude of mind rather than a prescribed set of practices. Nevertheless, it implies a fundamental reengineering of the mindset. It would be beyond the scope of this book to trace all the ramifications of this approach, but the main consequences for English language teaching can be summarised as follows:

- There are no truly valid grammar rules.
- There are no right answers.
- Words do not have fixed meanings.
- Language use is constantly changing.
- Context is more important than form.

Consequences for ELT

Implementing the fractal approach

The paradigm used in the fractal approach concentrates on creative output rather than on a fixed initial state of the language. Furthermore, it recognises that identical inputs may not produce identical outputs; an answer to a question that was valid yesterday may not be valid today. Meanings are in flux rather than fixed and are subject to external factors such as location, context and the identity of the speaker or writer. Since the model is rooted outside any notion of formal language structure, it may be counterintuitive to many language teachers, but also opens up new possibilities by:

Focus on creative output

121

- placing more emphasis on non-verbal contributors to meaning;
- acknowledging more grey areas of acceptability;
- stressing the fleeting nature of the spoken language;
- allowing you to use material you may previously have disregarded.

Guidelines for implementing the fractal approach in the ELT classroom

Implementing the fractal approach will take time and a certain amount of adjustment. However, there are a few things that teachers can do quite quickly in order to derive benefit for their students from these insights. In addition to being sensitive to change, there are a number of ways to ensure that you are teaching the language actually required for coping with specific real-life situations. So here are a few DOs and DON'Ts for implementing this approach in the classroom:

Don't

- sanitise the language in order to teach it;
- search for examples in order to prove a rule. If a rule does not work, throw it out;
- accept over-simplified models;
- reject real-life material by characterising it as 'slang', 'regional', 'jargon', 'telegram-style', 'colloquial' etc.

Happily, there are more DOs than DON'Ts.

Do

- focus on using real-world English in class;
- test grammar rules against experience before passing them on;
- emphasise the effect that context has on meaning;
- introduce new material from a wide range of sources, even if these conflict with one other;
- ensure that role plays are realistic rather than conform to a pre-set notion of what 'should' happen;
- encourage your students to explore new paths;

- provide your students with packages of ready-made real-life English, regardless of form;
- expand your own language skills by discovering new areas of English;
- concentrate on **what** you teach rather than on **how** you teach it.

This final point has become a recurring theme throughout this book, and I make no apologies for repeating this advice here. Getting the content right is so important that if readers were to seek one single 'take-home message' from these pages, this would probably be it. And the fractal approach takes this on board, too.

Final 'take-home message'

Whilst the fractal approach does not in itself present a quick fix to all classroom problems, it establishes the parameters for a **fundamental re-alignment of pedagogical priorities** in a way that is not only dynamic, but ultimately liberating.

References

Barnsley, M. (1988) *Fractals Everywhere*, Academic Press, Inc.

Becker, K., Dörfler, M. (1989) *Dynamical Systems and Fractals*, Cambridge University Press

Claypole, M. (2010) *The Fractal Approach to Teaching English as a Foreign Language*, Linguabooks/BOD

Peitgen, H., Saupe D. (ed.) 1988. *The Science of Fractal Images*, Springer-Verlag

Warnecke, H., Claypole M. (trans.) (1993) *The Fractal Company*, Springer-Verlag

http://webecoist.com/2008/09/07/17-amazing-examples-of-fractals-in-nature. Retrieved 09.12.2009

http://thesciencepundit.blogspot.com/2007_12_01_archive.html. Retrieved 09.12.2009

Acknowledgments

Thanks are due to the following for permission to reproduce copyright material and/or for their assistance or contributions during the preparation of the manuscript and the articles cited therein – or simply because their work was consulted during research. Further information on intellectual property rights is given on the copyright page at the front of this book.

Alpha College AG
Avatar English
British Broadcasting Corporation
Cambridge University Press
Channel 4
Deutsche Welle
Drive-Through ESL
Fox News
Half-Baked Software Inc.
International Association of Technical English Trainers (IATET)
Linden Research, Inc.
Linguaphone
Northern Songs
Oxford University Press
Royal Yachting Association
Sky News
SL English
SL Languages
Southern Sailing
Springer-Verlag
Tandem Hamburg
TechSmith Corporation
The consultants-e
Tianren Group
ver.di
Wieland Dental + Technik GmbH & Co KG

Further ELT titles from LinguaBooks

IN A STRANGE LAND
Short Stories for Creative Learning
Andrzej Cirocki and Alicia Peña Calvo   ISBN 978-3734789465

IN A STRANGE LAND is a collection of four original short stories which provide teachers with motivating and engaging classroom material at the CEFR B2 to C1 level and young adult learners with thought-provoking narratives and characters to whom they can relate.

This gripping teenage fiction encourages readers to use their imagination and interact with the texts in a variety of educational and experimental ways.

The stories are supported by creative tasks which enable students to integrate their various language skills, exploit computer technology, practise learning strategies and exercise autonomy.

Audio recordings of the stories are available on two CDs (available separately) which are suitable for classroom use and can also be listened to for pleasure.

The European Journal of Applied Linguistics and TEFL
Refereed academic journal
Edited by Andrzej Cirocki   ISSN 2192-1032

The European Journal of Applied Linguistics and TEFL (EJALTEFL) is a refereed academic publication published twice yearly to disseminate information, knowledge and expertise in applied linguistics with a special focus on English language teaching.

This provides a valuable source of reference for linguists, teacher trainers, materials developers and others in the field of EFL/ESL. Each issue offers key insights into current topics, broadening the reader's knowledge and promoting professional development.

For further information and to see the contents of the latest issue, go to http://www.linguabooks.com or visit the journal's dedicated website at http://theeuropeanjournal.eu.

Shortlisted for the 2016 ELTon Award for Innovation in Learner Resources

Academic Presenting and Presentations
A preparation course for university students
Peter Levrai and Averil Bolster   ISBN 978-3734783678

This practical training course is designed to help students cultivate academic presentation skills and deal with the variety of presentation tasks they may need to master during their studies.

The material is suitable for a global audience and can be used in a wide range of academic contexts since the content not only helps learners develop their presentation skills in English but also considers wider topics relevant to English for Academic Purposes, such as principles of research and the risk of plagiarism.

The accompanying online video presentations enable learners to immerse themselves still further in the material presented and witness first hand the impact of the techniques illustrated.

www.ingramcontent.com/pod-product-compliance
Lightning Source LLC
Chambersburg PA
CBHW070459090426
42735CB00012B/2619